C-1347   CAREER EXAMINATION SERIES

This is your
PASSBOOK for...

Lineman

Test Preparation Study Guide
Questions & Answers

NATIONAL LEARNING CORPORATION®

COPYRIGHT NOTICE

This book is SOLELY intended for, is sold ONLY to, and its use is RESTRICTED to individual, bona fide applicants or candidates who qualify by virtue of having seriously filed applications for appropriate license, certificate, professional and/or promotional advancement, higher school matriculation, scholarship, or other legitimate requirements of education and/or governmental authorities.

This book is NOT intended for use, class instruction, tutoring, training, duplication, copying, reprinting, excerption, or adaptation, etc., by:

1) Other publishers
2) Proprietors and/or Instructors of "Coaching" and/or Preparatory Courses
3) Personnel and/or Training Divisions of commercial, industrial, and governmental organizations
4) Schools, colleges, or universities and/or their departments and staffs, including teachers and other personnel
5) Testing Agencies or Bureaus
6) Study groups which seek by the purchase of a single volume to copy and/or duplicate and/or adapt this material for use by the group as a whole without having purchased individual volumes for each of the members of the group
7) Et al.

Such persons would be in violation of appropriate Federal and State statutes.

PROVISION OF LICENSING AGREEMENTS – Recognized educational, commercial, industrial, and governmental institutions and organizations, and others legitimately engaged in educational pursuits, including training, testing, and measurement activities, may address request for a licensing agreement to the copyright owners, who will determine whether, and under what conditions, including fees and charges, the materials in this book may be used them. In other words, a licensing facility exists for the legitimate use of the material in this book on other than an individual basis. However, it is asseverated and affirmed here that the material in this book CANNOT be used without the receipt of the express permission of such a licensing agreement from the Publishers. Inquiries re licensing should be addressed to the company, attention rights and permissions department.

All rights reserved, including the right of reproduction in whole or in part, in any form or by any means, electronic or mechanical, including photocopying, recording, or by any information storage and retrieval system, without permission in writing from the Publisher.

Copyright © 2024 by
National Learning Corporation

212 Michael Drive, Syosset, NY 11791
(516) 921-8888 • www.passbooks.com
E-mail: info@passbooks.com

PASSBOOK® SERIES

THE *PASSBOOK® SERIES* has been created to prepare applicants and candidates for the ultimate academic battlefield – the examination room.

At some time in our lives, each and every one of us may be required to take an examination – for validation, matriculation, admission, qualification, registration, certification, or licensure.

Based on the assumption that every applicant or candidate has met the basic formal educational standards, has taken the required number of courses, and read the necessary texts, the *PASSBOOK® SERIES* furnishes the one special preparation which may assure passing with confidence, instead of failing with insecurity. Examination questions – together with answers – are furnished as the basic vehicle for study so that the mysteries of the examination and its compounding difficulties may be eliminated or diminished by a sure method.

This book is meant to help you pass your examination provided that you qualify and are serious in your objective.

The entire field is reviewed through the huge store of content information which is succinctly presented through a provocative and challenging approach – the question-and-answer method.

A climate of success is established by furnishing the correct answers at the end of each test.

You soon learn to recognize types of questions, forms of questions, and patterns of questioning. You may even begin to anticipate expected outcomes.

You perceive that many questions are repeated or adapted so that you can gain acute insights, which may enable you to score many sure points.

You learn how to confront new questions, or types of questions, and to attack them confidently and work out the correct answers.

You note objectives and emphases, and recognize pitfalls and dangers, so that you may make positive educational adjustments.

Moreover, you are kept fully informed in relation to new concepts, methods, practices, and directions in the field.

You discover that you are actually taking the examination all the time: you are preparing for the examination by "taking" an examination, not by reading extraneous and/or supererogatory textbooks.

In short, this PASSBOOK®, used directedly, should be an important factor in helping you to pass your test.

LINEMAN

DUTIES
This is electrical work consisting of the erection, installation and maintenance of all overhead and underground electric power distribution lines. Work requires climbing of poles in all kinds of weather conditions and rigid observance of safety precautions to prevent injury to lineman, linemen helpers and by-standers. Supervision may be exercised over several helpers and laborers.

This classification covers the construction, installation, alteration, maintenance or repair of an electrical wiring system, including sub-stations or components thereof, which is or is intended to be owned, operated and maintained by an electric power supplier such as a public or private utility, a utility cooperative, or any other property franchised electric power supplier, for the purpose of furnishing electrical services to one or more customers. Linemen may perform related duties as required.

EXAMPLES OF WORK:
Digs holes, sets and guys poles for electric power transmission wires;
Strings eletrical power lines on poles and through underground conduits;
Installs cross arms and erects transformers on power poles;
Repairs damage done to electric transmission lines by storms;
Trims and prunes trees in the path of transmission cables;
Installs and maintains street lighting fixtures;
Runs service lines from transformers on poles to homes and buildings;
Installs cutouts, fuses, electric lights, arresters, and insulators and transformers;
Repairs and tests meters:
Prepares reocrds of jobs and job time sheets;
Keeps inventories of supplies and materials in stock and used on jobs.

REQUIRED KNOWLEDGES, SKILLS AND ABILITIES:
Good knowledge of theory and principles of electricity and electrical distribution systems as they relate to duties; good knowledge of standard safety measures and devices in handling high voltage electrical circuits; ability to use tools and equipment of the trade; ability to follow oral and written instructions; ability to climb poles and towers; ability to splice wires and cables; steady nerves; physical strength and stamina to perform arduous manual labor and to withstand adverse weather conditions.

TEST
The written test will be designed to test for knowledge, skills, and/or abilities in such areas as: Basic principles of electricity; tools of the electrical trade; operation of mechanical and electrical devices; installation and maintenance of electrical distribution pole lines; knowledge of transformers, conductors, overhead lines, underground lines, equipment and safety, grounding methods, service drops and laterals, poles and structures, and electric supply stations.

HOW TO TAKE A TEST

I. YOU MUST PASS AN EXAMINATION

A. *WHAT EVERY CANDIDATE SHOULD KNOW*

Examination applicants often ask us for help in preparing for the written test. What can I study in advance? What kinds of questions will be asked? How will the test be given? How will the papers be graded?

As an applicant for a civil service examination, you may be wondering about some of these things. Our purpose here is to suggest effective methods of advance study and to describe civil service examinations.

Your chances for success on this examination can be increased if you know how to prepare. Those "pre-examination jitters" can be reduced if you know what to expect. You can even experience an adventure in good citizenship if you know why civil service exams are given.

B. *WHY ARE CIVIL SERVICE EXAMINATIONS GIVEN?*

Civil service examinations are important to you in two ways. As a citizen, you want public jobs filled by employees who know how to do their work. As a job seeker, you want a fair chance to compete for that job on an equal footing with other candidates. The best-known means of accomplishing this two-fold goal is the competitive examination.

Exams are widely publicized throughout the nation. They may be administered for jobs in federal, state, city, municipal, town or village governments or agencies.

Any citizen may apply, with some limitations, such as the age or residence of applicants. Your experience and education may be reviewed to see whether you meet the requirements for the particular examination. When these requirements exist, they are reasonable and applied consistently to all applicants. Thus, a competitive examination may cause you some uneasiness now, but it is your privilege and safeguard.

C. *HOW ARE CIVIL SERVICE EXAMS DEVELOPED?*

Examinations are carefully written by trained technicians who are specialists in the field known as "psychological measurement," in consultation with recognized authorities in the field of work that the test will cover. These experts recommend the subject matter areas or skills to be tested; only those knowledges or skills important to your success on the job are included. The most reliable books and source materials available are used as references. Together, the experts and technicians judge the difficulty level of the questions.

Test technicians know how to phrase questions so that the problem is clearly stated. Their ethics do not permit "trick" or "catch" questions. Questions may have been tried out on sample groups, or subjected to statistical analysis, to determine their usefulness.

Written tests are often used in combination with performance tests, ratings of training and experience, and oral interviews. All of these measures combine to form the best-known means of finding the right person for the right job.

II. HOW TO PASS THE WRITTEN TEST

A. NATURE OF THE EXAMINATION

To prepare intelligently for civil service examinations, you should know how they differ from school examinations you have taken. In school you were assigned certain definite pages to read or subjects to cover. The examination questions were quite detailed and usually emphasized memory. Civil service exams, on the other hand, try to discover your present ability to perform the duties of a position, plus your potentiality to learn these duties. In other words, a civil service exam attempts to predict how successful you will be. Questions cover such a broad area that they cannot be as minute and detailed as school exam questions.

In the public service similar kinds of work, or positions, are grouped together in one "class." This process is known as *position-classification*. All the positions in a class are paid according to the salary range for that class. One class title covers all of these positions, and they are all tested by the same examination.

B. FOUR BASIC STEPS

1) Study the announcement

How, then, can you know what subjects to study? Our best answer is: "Learn as much as possible about the class of positions for which you've applied." The exam will test the knowledge, skills and abilities needed to do the work.

Your most valuable source of information about the position you want is the official exam announcement. This announcement lists the training and experience qualifications. Check these standards and apply only if you come reasonably close to meeting them.

The brief description of the position in the examination announcement offers some clues to the subjects which will be tested. Think about the job itself. Review the duties in your mind. Can you perform them, or are there some in which you are rusty? Fill in the blank spots in your preparation.

Many jurisdictions preview the written test in the exam announcement by including a section called "Knowledge and Abilities Required," "Scope of the Examination," or some similar heading. Here you will find out specifically what fields will be tested.

2) Review your own background

Once you learn in general what the position is all about, and what you need to know to do the work, ask yourself which subjects you already know fairly well and which need improvement. You may wonder whether to concentrate on improving your strong areas or on building some background in your fields of weakness. When the announcement has specified "some knowledge" or "considerable knowledge," or has used adjectives like "beginning principles of..." or "advanced ... methods," you can get a clue as to the number and difficulty of questions to be asked in any given field. More questions, and hence broader coverage, would be included for those subjects which are more important in the work. Now weigh your strengths and weaknesses against the job requirements and prepare accordingly.

3) Determine the level of the position

Another way to tell how intensively you should prepare is to understand the level of the job for which you are applying. Is it the entering level? In other words, is this the position in which beginners in a field of work are hired? Or is it an intermediate or advanced level? Sometimes this is indicated by such words as "Junior" or "Senior" in the class title. Other jurisdictions use Roman numerals to designate the level – Clerk I, Clerk II, for example. The word "Supervisor" sometimes appears in the title. If the level is not indicated by the title, check the description of duties. Will you be working under very close supervision, or will you have responsibility for independent decisions in this work?

4) Choose appropriate study materials

Now that you know the subjects to be examined and the relative amount of each subject to be covered, you can choose suitable study materials. For beginning level jobs, or even advanced ones, if you have a pronounced weakness in some aspect of your training, read a modern, standard textbook in that field. Be sure it is up to date and has general coverage. Such books are normally available at your library, and the librarian will be glad to help you locate one. For entry-level positions, questions of appropriate difficulty are chosen – neither highly advanced questions, nor those too simple. Such questions require careful thought but not advanced training.

If the position for which you are applying is technical or advanced, you will read more advanced, specialized material. If you are already familiar with the basic principles of your field, elementary textbooks would waste your time. Concentrate on advanced textbooks and technical periodicals. Think through the concepts and review difficult problems in your field.

These are all general sources. You can get more ideas on your own initiative, following these leads. For example, training manuals and publications of the government agency which employs workers in your field can be useful, particularly for technical and professional positions. A letter or visit to the government department involved may result in more specific study suggestions, and certainly will provide you with a more definite idea of the exact nature of the position you are seeking.

III. KINDS OF TESTS

Tests are used for purposes other than measuring knowledge and ability to perform specified duties. For some positions, it is equally important to test ability to make adjustments to new situations or to profit from training. In others, basic mental abilities not dependent on information are essential. Questions which test these things may not appear as pertinent to the duties of the position as those which test for knowledge and information. Yet they are often highly important parts of a fair examination. For very general questions, it is almost impossible to help you direct your study efforts. What we can do is to point out some of the more common of these general abilities needed in public service positions and describe some typical questions.

1) General information

Broad, general information has been found useful for predicting job success in some kinds of work. This is tested in a variety of ways, from vocabulary lists to questions about current events. Basic background in some field of work, such as sociology or economics, may be sampled in a group of questions. Often these are principles which have become familiar to most persons through exposure rather than through formal training. It is difficult to advise you how to study for these questions; being alert to the world around you is our best suggestion.

2) Verbal ability

An example of an ability needed in many positions is verbal or language ability. Verbal ability is, in brief, the ability to use and understand words. Vocabulary and grammar tests are typical measures of this ability. Reading comprehension or paragraph interpretation questions are common in many kinds of civil service tests. You are given a paragraph of written material and asked to find its central meaning.

3) Numerical ability

Number skills can be tested by the familiar arithmetic problem, by checking paired lists of numbers to see which are alike and which are different, or by interpreting charts and graphs. In the latter test, a graph may be printed in the test booklet which you are asked to use as the basis for answering questions.

4) Observation

A popular test for law-enforcement positions is the observation test. A picture is shown to you for several minutes, then taken away. Questions about the picture test your ability to observe both details and larger elements.

5) Following directions

In many positions in the public service, the employee must be able to carry out written instructions dependably and accurately. You may be given a chart with several columns, each column listing a variety of information. The questions require you to carry out directions involving the information given in the chart.

6) Skills and aptitudes

Performance tests effectively measure some manual skills and aptitudes. When the skill is one in which you are trained, such as typing or shorthand, you can practice. These tests are often very much like those given in business school or high school courses. For many of the other skills and aptitudes, however, no short-time preparation can be made. Skills and abilities natural to you or that you have developed throughout your lifetime are being tested.

Many of the general questions just described provide all the data needed to answer the questions and ask you to use your reasoning ability to find the answers. Your best preparation for these tests, as well as for tests of facts and ideas, is to be at your physical and mental best. You, no doubt, have your own methods of getting into an exam-taking mood and keeping "in shape." The next section lists some ideas on this subject.

IV. KINDS OF QUESTIONS

Only rarely is the "essay" question, which you answer in narrative form, used in civil service tests. Civil service tests are usually of the short-answer type. Full instructions for answering these questions will be given to you at the examination. But in case this is your first experience with short-answer questions and separate answer sheets, here is what you need to know:

1) Multiple-choice Questions

Most popular of the short-answer questions is the "multiple choice" or "best answer" question. It can be used, for example, to test for factual knowledge, ability to solve problems or judgment in meeting situations found at work.

A multiple-choice question is normally one of three types—
- It can begin with an incomplete statement followed by several possible endings. You are to find the one ending which *best* completes the statement, although some of the others may not be entirely wrong.
- It can also be a complete statement in the form of a question which is answered by choosing one of the statements listed.

- It can be in the form of a problem – again you select the best answer.

Here is an example of a multiple-choice question with a discussion which should give you some clues as to the method for choosing the right answer:

When an employee has a complaint about his assignment, the action which will *best* help him overcome his difficulty is to
    A. discuss his difficulty with his coworkers
    B. take the problem to the head of the organization
    C. take the problem to the person who gave him the assignment
    D. say nothing to anyone about his complaint

In answering this question, you should study each of the choices to find which is best. Consider choice "A" – Certainly an employee may discuss his complaint with fellow employees, but no change or improvement can result, and the complaint remains unresolved. Choice "B" is a poor choice since the head of the organization probably does not know what assignment you have been given, and taking your problem to him is known as "going over the head" of the supervisor. The supervisor, or person who made the assignment, is the person who can clarify it or correct any injustice. Choice "C" is, therefore, correct. To say nothing, as in choice "D," is unwise. Supervisors have and interest in knowing the problems employees are facing, and the employee is seeking a solution to his problem.

2) True/False Questions

The "true/false" or "right/wrong" form of question is sometimes used. Here a complete statement is given. Your job is to decide whether the statement is right or wrong.

SAMPLE: A roaming cell-phone call to a nearby city costs less than a non-roaming call to a distant city.

This statement is wrong, or false, since roaming calls are more expensive.

This is not a complete list of all possible question forms, although most of the others are variations of these common types. You will always get complete directions for answering questions. Be sure you understand *how* to mark your answers – ask questions until you do.

V. RECORDING YOUR ANSWERS

Computer terminals are used more and more today for many different kinds of exams.
For an examination with very few applicants, you may be told to record your answers in the test booklet itself. Separate answer sheets are much more common. If this separate answer sheet is to be scored by machine – and this is often the case – it is highly important that you mark your answers correctly in order to get credit.
An electronic scoring machine is often used in civil service offices because of the speed with which papers can be scored. Machine-scored answer sheets must be marked with a pencil, which will be given to you. This pencil has a high graphite content which responds to the electronic scoring machine. As a matter of fact, stray dots may register as answers, so do not let your pencil rest on the answer sheet while you are pondering the correct answer. Also, if your pencil lead breaks or is otherwise defective, ask for another.

Since the answer sheet will be dropped in a slot in the scoring machine, be careful not to bend the corners or get the paper crumpled.

The answer sheet normally has five vertical columns of numbers, with 30 numbers to a column. These numbers correspond to the question numbers in your test booklet. After each number, going across the page are four or five pairs of dotted lines. These short dotted lines have small letters or numbers above them. The first two pairs may also have a "T" or "F" above the letters. This indicates that the first two pairs only are to be used if the questions are of the true-false type. If the questions are multiple choice, disregard the "T" and "F" and pay attention only to the small letters or numbers.

Answer your questions in the manner of the sample that follows:

32. The largest city in the United States is
    A. Washington, D.C.
    B. New York City
    C. Chicago
    D. Detroit
    E. San Francisco

1) Choose the answer you think is best. (New York City is the largest, so "B" is correct.)
2) Find the row of dotted lines numbered the same as the question you are answering. (Find row number 32)
3) Find the pair of dotted lines corresponding to the answer. (Find the pair of lines under the mark "B.")
4) Make a solid black mark between the dotted lines.

VI. BEFORE THE TEST

Common sense will help you find procedures to follow to get ready for an examination. Too many of us, however, overlook these sensible measures. Indeed, nervousness and fatigue have been found to be the most serious reasons why applicants fail to do their best on civil service tests. Here is a list of reminders:

- Begin your preparation early – Don't wait until the last minute to go scurrying around for books and materials or to find out what the position is all about.
- Prepare continuously – An hour a night for a week is better than an all-night cram session. This has been definitely established. What is more, a night a week for a month will return better dividends than crowding your study into a shorter period of time.
- Locate the place of the exam – You have been sent a notice telling you when and where to report for the examination. If the location is in a different town or otherwise unfamiliar to you, it would be well to inquire the best route and learn something about the building.
- Relax the night before the test – Allow your mind to rest. Do not study at all that night. Plan some mild recreation or diversion; then go to bed early and get a good night's sleep.
- Get up early enough to make a leisurely trip to the place for the test – This way unforeseen events, traffic snarls, unfamiliar buildings, etc. will not upset you.
- Dress comfortably – A written test is not a fashion show. You will be known by number and not by name, so wear something comfortable.

- Leave excess paraphernalia at home – Shopping bags and odd bundles will get in your way. You need bring only the items mentioned in the official notice you received; usually everything you need is provided. Do not bring reference books to the exam. They will only confuse those last minutes and be taken away from you when in the test room.
- Arrive somewhat ahead of time – If because of transportation schedules you must get there very early, bring a newspaper or magazine to take your mind off yourself while waiting.
- Locate the examination room – When you have found the proper room, you will be directed to the seat or part of the room where you will sit. Sometimes you are given a sheet of instructions to read while you are waiting. Do not fill out any forms until you are told to do so; just read them and be prepared.
- Relax and prepare to listen to the instructions
- If you have any physical problem that may keep you from doing your best, be sure to tell the test administrator. If you are sick or in poor health, you really cannot do your best on the exam. You can come back and take the test some other time.

VII. AT THE TEST

The day of the test is here and you have the test booklet in your hand. The temptation to get going is very strong. Caution! There is more to success than knowing the right answers. You must know how to identify your papers and understand variations in the type of short-answer question used in this particular examination. Follow these suggestions for maximum results from your efforts:

1) Cooperate with the monitor

The test administrator has a duty to create a situation in which you can be as much at ease as possible. He will give instructions, tell you when to begin, check to see that you are marking your answer sheet correctly, and so on. He is not there to guard you, although he will see that your competitors do not take unfair advantage. He wants to help you do your best.

2) Listen to all instructions

Don't jump the gun! Wait until you understand all directions. In most civil service tests you get more time than you need to answer the questions. So don't be in a hurry. Read each word of instructions until you clearly understand the meaning. Study the examples, listen to all announcements and follow directions. Ask questions if you do not understand what to do.

3) Identify your papers

Civil service exams are usually identified by number only. You will be assigned a number; you must not put your name on your test papers. Be sure to copy your number correctly. Since more than one exam may be given, copy your exact examination title.

4) Plan your time

Unless you are told that a test is a "speed" or "rate of work" test, speed itself is usually not important. Time enough to answer all the questions will be provided, but this does not mean that you have all day. An overall time limit has been set. Divide the total time (in minutes) by the number of questions to determine the approximate time you have for each question.

5) Do not linger over difficult questions

If you come across a difficult question, mark it with a paper clip (useful to have along) and come back to it when you have been through the booklet. One caution if you do this – be sure to skip a number on your answer sheet as well. Check often to be sure that you have not lost your place and that you are marking in the row numbered the same as the question you are answering.

6) Read the questions

Be sure you know what the question asks! Many capable people are unsuccessful because they failed to *read* the questions correctly.

7) Answer all questions

Unless you have been instructed that a penalty will be deducted for incorrect answers, it is better to guess than to omit a question.

8) Speed tests

It is often better NOT to guess on speed tests. It has been found that on timed tests people are tempted to spend the last few seconds before time is called in marking answers at random – without even reading them – in the hope of picking up a few extra points. To discourage this practice, the instructions may warn you that your score will be "corrected" for guessing. That is, a penalty will be applied. The incorrect answers will be deducted from the correct ones, or some other penalty formula will be used.

9) Review your answers

If you finish before time is called, go back to the questions you guessed or omitted to give them further thought. Review other answers if you have time.

10) Return your test materials

If you are ready to leave before others have finished or time is called, take ALL your materials to the monitor and leave quietly. Never take any test material with you. The monitor can discover whose papers are not complete, and taking a test booklet may be grounds for disqualification.

VIII. EXAMINATION TECHNIQUES

1) Read the general instructions carefully. These are usually printed on the first page of the exam booklet. As a rule, these instructions refer to the timing of the examination; the fact that you should not start work until the signal and must stop work at a signal, etc. If there are any *special* instructions, such as a choice of questions to be answered, make sure that you note this instruction carefully.

2) When you are ready to start work on the examination, that is as soon as the signal has been given, read the instructions to each question booklet, underline any key words or phrases, such as *least, best, outline, describe* and the like. In this way you will tend to answer as requested rather than discover on reviewing your paper that you *listed without describing*, that you selected the *worst* choice rather than the *best* choice, etc.

3) If the examination is of the objective or multiple-choice type – that is, each question will also give a series of possible answers: A, B, C or D, and you are called upon to select the best answer and write the letter next to that answer on your answer paper – it is advisable to start answering each question in turn. There may be anywhere from 50 to 100 such questions in the three or four hours allotted and you can see how much time would be taken if you read through all the questions before beginning to answer any. Furthermore, if you come across a question or group of questions which you know would be difficult to answer, it would undoubtedly affect your handling of all the other questions.

4) If the examination is of the essay type and contains but a few questions, it is a moot point as to whether you should read all the questions before starting to answer any one. Of course, if you are given a choice – say five out of seven and the like – then it is essential to read all the questions so you can eliminate the two that are most difficult. If, however, you are asked to answer all the questions, there may be danger in trying to answer the easiest one first because you may find that you will spend too much time on it. The best technique is to answer the first question, then proceed to the second, etc.

5) Time your answers. Before the exam begins, write down the time it started, then add the time allowed for the examination and write down the time it must be completed, then divide the time available somewhat as follows:
   - If 3-1/2 hours are allowed, that would be 210 minutes. If you have 80 objective-type questions, that would be an average of 2-1/2 minutes per question. Allow yourself no more than 2 minutes per question, or a total of 160 minutes, which will permit about 50 minutes to review.
   - If for the time allotment of 210 minutes there are 7 essay questions to answer, that would average about 30 minutes a question. Give yourself only 25 minutes per question so that you have about 35 minutes to review.

6) The most important instruction is to *read each question* and make sure you know what is wanted. The second most important instruction is to *time yourself properly* so that you answer every question. The third most important instruction is to *answer every question*. Guess if you have to but include something for each question. Remember that you will receive no credit for a blank and will probably receive some credit if you write something in answer to an essay question. If you guess a letter – say "B" for a multiple-choice question – you may have guessed right. If you leave a blank as an answer to a multiple-choice question, the examiners may respect your feelings but it will not add a point to your score. Some exams may penalize you for wrong answers, so in such cases *only*, you may not want to guess unless you have some basis for your answer.

7) Suggestions
   a. Objective-type questions
      1. Examine the question booklet for proper sequence of pages and questions
      2. Read all instructions carefully
      3. Skip any question which seems too difficult; return to it after all other questions have been answered
      4. Apportion your time properly; do not spend too much time on any single question or group of questions

5. Note and underline key words – *all, most, fewest, least, best, worst, same, opposite,* etc.
6. Pay particular attention to negatives
7. Note unusual option, e.g., unduly long, short, complex, different or similar in content to the body of the question
8. Observe the use of "hedging" words – *probably, may, most likely,* etc.
9. Make sure that your answer is put next to the same number as the question
10. Do not second-guess unless you have good reason to believe the second answer is definitely more correct
11. Cross out original answer if you decide another answer is more accurate; do not erase until you are ready to hand your paper in
12. Answer all questions; guess unless instructed otherwise
13. Leave time for review

b. Essay questions
1. Read each question carefully
2. Determine exactly what is wanted. Underline key words or phrases.
3. Decide on outline or paragraph answer
4. Include many different points and elements unless asked to develop any one or two points or elements
5. Show impartiality by giving pros and cons unless directed to select one side only
6. Make and write down any assumptions you find necessary to answer the questions
7. Watch your English, grammar, punctuation and choice of words
8. Time your answers; don't crowd material

8) Answering the essay question

Most essay questions can be answered by framing the specific response around several key words or ideas. Here are a few such key words or ideas:

M's: manpower, materials, methods, money, management
P's: purpose, program, policy, plan, procedure, practice, problems, pitfalls, personnel, public relations

a. Six basic steps in handling problems:
1. Preliminary plan and background development
2. Collect information, data and facts
3. Analyze and interpret information, data and facts
4. Analyze and develop solutions as well as make recommendations
5. Prepare report and sell recommendations
6. Install recommendations and follow up effectiveness

b. Pitfalls to avoid
1. *Taking things for granted* – A statement of the situation does not necessarily imply that each of the elements is necessarily true; for example, a complaint may be invalid and biased so that all that can be taken for granted is that a complaint has been registered

2. *Considering only one side of a situation* – Wherever possible, indicate several alternatives and then point out the reasons you selected the best one
3. *Failing to indicate follow up* – Whenever your answer indicates action on your part, make certain that you will take proper follow-up action to see how successful your recommendations, procedures or actions turn out to be
4. *Taking too long in answering any single question* – Remember to time your answers properly

IX. AFTER THE TEST

Scoring procedures differ in detail among civil service jurisdictions although the general principles are the same. Whether the papers are hand-scored or graded by machine we have described, they are nearly always graded by number. That is, the person who marks the paper knows only the number – never the name – of the applicant. Not until all the papers have been graded will they be matched with names. If other tests, such as training and experience or oral interview ratings have been given, scores will be combined. Different parts of the examination usually have different weights. For example, the written test might count 60 percent of the final grade, and a rating of training and experience 40 percent. In many jurisdictions, veterans will have a certain number of points added to their grades.

After the final grade has been determined, the names are placed in grade order and an eligible list is established. There are various methods for resolving ties between those who get the same final grade – probably the most common is to place first the name of the person whose application was received first. Job offers are made from the eligible list in the order the names appear on it. You will be notified of your grade and your rank as soon as all these computations have been made. This will be done as rapidly as possible.

People who are found to meet the requirements in the announcement are called "eligibles." Their names are put on a list of eligible candidates. An eligible's chances of getting a job depend on how high he stands on this list and how fast agencies are filling jobs from the list.

When a job is to be filled from a list of eligibles, the agency asks for the names of people on the list of eligibles for that job. When the civil service commission receives this request, it sends to the agency the names of the three people highest on this list. Or, if the job to be filled has specialized requirements, the office sends the agency the names of the top three persons who meet these requirements from the general list.

The appointing officer makes a choice from among the three people whose names were sent to him. If the selected person accepts the appointment, the names of the others are put back on the list to be considered for future openings.

That is the rule in hiring from all kinds of eligible lists, whether they are for typist, carpenter, chemist, or something else. For every vacancy, the appointing officer has his choice of any one of the top three eligibles on the list. This explains why the person whose name is on top of the list sometimes does not get an appointment when some of the persons lower on the list do. If the appointing officer chooses the second or third eligible, the No. 1 eligible does not get a job at once, but stays on the list until he is appointed or the list is terminated.

X. HOW TO PASS THE INTERVIEW TEST

The examination for which you applied requires an oral interview test. You have already taken the written test and you are now being called for the interview test – the final part of the formal examination.

You may think that it is not possible to prepare for an interview test and that there are no procedures to follow during an interview. Our purpose is to point out some things you can do in advance that will help you and some good rules to follow and pitfalls to avoid while you are being interviewed.

What is an interview supposed to test?

The written examination is designed to test the technical knowledge and competence of the candidate; the oral is designed to evaluate intangible qualities, not readily measured otherwise, and to establish a list showing the relative fitness of each candidate – as measured against his competitors – for the position sought. Scoring is not on the basis of "right" and "wrong," but on a sliding scale of values ranging from "not passable" to "outstanding." As a matter of fact, it is possible to achieve a relatively low score without a single "incorrect" answer because of evident weakness in the qualities being measured.

Occasionally, an examination may consist entirely of an oral test – either an individual or a group oral. In such cases, information is sought concerning the technical knowledges and abilities of the candidate, since there has been no written examination for this purpose. More commonly, however, an oral test is used to supplement a written examination.

Who conducts interviews?

The composition of oral boards varies among different jurisdictions. In nearly all, a representative of the personnel department serves as chairman. One of the members of the board may be a representative of the department in which the candidate would work. In some cases, "outside experts" are used, and, frequently, a businessman or some other representative of the general public is asked to serve. Labor and management or other special groups may be represented. The aim is to secure the services of experts in the appropriate field.

However the board is composed, it is a good idea (and not at all improper or unethical) to ascertain in advance of the interview who the members are and what groups they represent. When you are introduced to them, you will have some idea of their backgrounds and interests, and at least you will not stutter and stammer over their names.

What should be done before the interview?

While knowledge about the board members is useful and takes some of the surprise element out of the interview, there is other preparation which is more substantive. It *is* possible to prepare for an oral interview – in several ways:

1) Keep a copy of your application and review it carefully before the interview

This may be the only document before the oral board, and the starting point of the interview. Know what education and experience you have listed there, and the sequence and dates of all of it. Sometimes the board will ask you to review the highlights of your experience for them; you should not have to hem and haw doing it.

2) Study the class specification and the examination announcement

Usually, the oral board has one or both of these to guide them. The qualities, characteristics or knowledges required by the position sought are stated in these documents. They offer valuable clues as to the nature of the oral interview. For example, if the job involves supervisory responsibilities, the announcement will usually indicate that knowledge of modern supervisory methods and the qualifications of the candidate as a supervisor will be tested. If so, you can expect such questions, frequently in the form of a hypothetical situation which you are expected to solve. NEVER go into an oral without knowledge of the duties and responsibilities of the job you seek.

3) Think through each qualification required

Try to visualize the kind of questions you would ask if you were a board member. How well could you answer them? Try especially to appraise your own knowledge and background in each area, *measured against the job sought*, and identify any areas in which you are weak. Be critical and realistic – do not flatter yourself.

4) Do some general reading in areas in which you feel you may be weak

For example, if the job involves supervision and your past experience has NOT, some general reading in supervisory methods and practices, particularly in the field of human relations, might be useful. Do NOT study agency procedures or detailed manuals. The oral board will be testing your understanding and capacity, not your memory.

5) Get a good night's sleep and watch your general health and mental attitude

You will want a clear head at the interview. Take care of a cold or any other minor ailment, and of course, no hangovers.

What should be done on the day of the interview?

Now comes the day of the interview itself. Give yourself plenty of time to get there. Plan to arrive somewhat ahead of the scheduled time, particularly if your appointment is in the fore part of the day. If a previous candidate fails to appear, the board might be ready for you a bit early. By early afternoon an oral board is almost invariably behind schedule if there are many candidates, and you may have to wait. Take along a book or magazine to read, or your application to review, but leave any extraneous material in the waiting room when you go in for your interview. In any event, relax and compose yourself.

The matter of dress is important. The board is forming impressions about you – from your experience, your manners, your attitude, and your appearance. Give your personal appearance careful attention. Dress your best, but not your flashiest. Choose conservative, appropriate clothing, and be sure it is immaculate. This is a business interview, and your appearance should indicate that you regard it as such. Besides, being well groomed and properly dressed will help boost your confidence.

Sooner or later, someone will call your name and escort you into the interview room. *This is it.* From here on you are on your own. It is too late for any more preparation. But remember, you asked for this opportunity to prove your fitness, and you are here because your request was granted.

What happens when you go in?

The usual sequence of events will be as follows: The clerk (who is often the board stenographer) will introduce you to the chairman of the oral board, who will introduce you to the other members of the board. Acknowledge the introductions before you sit down. Do not be surprised if you find a microphone facing you or a stenotypist sitting by. Oral interviews are usually recorded in the event of an appeal or other review.

Usually the chairman of the board will open the interview by reviewing the highlights of your education and work experience from your application – primarily for the benefit of the other members of the board, as well as to get the material into the record. Do not interrupt or comment unless there is an error or significant misinterpretation; if that is the case, do not hesitate. But do not quibble about insignificant matters. Also, he will usually ask you some question about your education, experience or your present job – partly to get you to start talking and to establish the interviewing "rapport." He may start the actual questioning, or turn it over to one of the other members. Frequently, each member undertakes the questioning on a particular area, one in which he is perhaps most competent, so you can expect each member to participate in the examination. Because time is limited, you may also expect some rather abrupt switches in the direction the questioning takes, so do not be upset by it. Normally, a board member will not pursue a single line of questioning unless he discovers a particular strength or weakness.

After each member has participated, the chairman will usually ask whether any member has any further questions, then will ask you if you have anything you wish to add. Unless you are expecting this question, it may floor you. Worse, it may start you off on an extended, extemporaneous speech. The board is not usually seeking more information. The question is principally to offer you a last opportunity to present further qualifications or to indicate that you have nothing to add. So, if you feel that a significant qualification or characteristic has been overlooked, it is proper to point it out in a sentence or so. Do not compliment the board on the thoroughness of their examination – they have been sketchy, and you know it. If you wish, merely say, "No thank you, I have nothing further to add." This is a point where you can "talk yourself out" of a good impression or fail to present an important bit of information. Remember, *you close the interview yourself*.

The chairman will then say, "That is all, Mr. _____, thank you." Do not be startled; the interview is over, and quicker than you think. Thank him, gather your belongings and take your leave. Save your sigh of relief for the other side of the door.

How to put your best foot forward
Throughout this entire process, you may feel that the board individually and collectively is trying to pierce your defenses, seek out your hidden weaknesses and embarrass and confuse you. Actually, this is not true. They are obliged to make an appraisal of your qualifications for the job you are seeking, and they want to see you in your best light. Remember, they must interview all candidates and a non-cooperative candidate may become a failure in spite of their best efforts to bring out his qualifications. Here are 15 suggestions that will help you:

1) Be natural – Keep your attitude confident, not cocky
If you are not confident that you can do the job, do not expect the board to be. Do not apologize for your weaknesses, try to bring out your strong points. The board is interested in a positive, not negative, presentation. Cockiness will antagonize any board member and make him wonder if you are covering up a weakness by a false show of strength.

2) Get comfortable, but don't lounge or sprawl
Sit erectly but not stiffly. A careless posture may lead the board to conclude that you are careless in other things, or at least that you are not impressed by the importance of the occasion. Either conclusion is natural, even if incorrect. Do not fuss with your clothing, a pencil or an ashtray. Your hands may occasionally be useful to emphasize a point; do not let them become a point of distraction.

3) Do not wisecrack or make small talk
This is a serious situation, and your attitude should show that you consider it as such. Further, the time of the board is limited – they do not want to waste it, and neither should you.

4) Do not exaggerate your experience or abilities

In the first place, from information in the application or other interviews and sources, the board may know more about you than you think. Secondly, you probably will not get away with it. An experienced board is rather adept at spotting such a situation, so do not take the chance.

5) If you know a board member, do not make a point of it, yet do not hide it

Certainly you are not fooling him, and probably not the other members of the board. Do not try to take advantage of your acquaintanceship – it will probably do you little good.

6) Do not dominate the interview

Let the board do that. They will give you the clues – do not assume that you have to do all the talking. Realize that the board has a number of questions to ask you, and do not try to take up all the interview time by showing off your extensive knowledge of the answer to the first one.

7) Be attentive

You only have 20 minutes or so, and you should keep your attention at its sharpest throughout. When a member is addressing a problem or question to you, give him your undivided attention. Address your reply principally to him, but do not exclude the other board members.

8) Do not interrupt

A board member may be stating a problem for you to analyze. He will ask you a question when the time comes. Let him state the problem, and wait for the question.

9) Make sure you understand the question

Do not try to answer until you are sure what the question is. If it is not clear, restate it in your own words or ask the board member to clarify it for you. However, do not haggle about minor elements.

10) Reply promptly but not hastily

A common entry on oral board rating sheets is "candidate responded readily," or "candidate hesitated in replies." Respond as promptly and quickly as you can, but do not jump to a hasty, ill-considered answer.

11) Do not be peremptory in your answers

A brief answer is proper – but do not fire your answer back. That is a losing game from your point of view. The board member can probably ask questions much faster than you can answer them.

12) Do not try to create the answer you think the board member wants

He is interested in what kind of mind you have and how it works – not in playing games. Furthermore, he can usually spot this practice and will actually grade you down on it.

13) Do not switch sides in your reply merely to agree with a board member

Frequently, a member will take a contrary position merely to draw you out and to see if you are willing and able to defend your point of view. Do not start a debate, yet do not surrender a good position. If a position is worth taking, it is worth defending.

14) Do not be afraid to admit an error in judgment if you are shown to be wrong
The board knows that you are forced to reply without any opportunity for careful consideration. Your answer may be demonstrably wrong. If so, admit it and get on with the interview.

15) Do not dwell at length on your present job
The opening question may relate to your present assignment. Answer the question but do not go into an extended discussion. You are being examined for a *new* job, not your present one. As a matter of fact, try to phrase ALL your answers in terms of the job for which you are being examined.

Basis of Rating
Probably you will forget most of these "do's" and "don'ts" when you walk into the oral interview room. Even remembering them all will not ensure you a passing grade. Perhaps you did not have the qualifications in the first place. But remembering them will help you to put your best foot forward, without treading on the toes of the board members.

Rumor and popular opinion to the contrary notwithstanding, an oral board wants you to make the best appearance possible. They know you are under pressure – but they also want to see how you respond to it as a guide to what your reaction would be under the pressures of the job you seek. They will be influenced by the degree of poise you display, the personal traits you show and the manner in which you respond.

ABOUT THIS BOOK

This book contains tests divided into Examination Sections. Go through each test, answering every question in the margin. We have also attached a sample answer sheet at the back of the book that can be removed and used. At the end of each test look at the answer key and check your answers. On the ones you got wrong, look at the right answer choice and learn. Do not fill in the answers first. Do not memorize the questions and answers, but understand the answer and principles involved. On your test, the questions will likely be different from the samples. Questions are changed and new ones added. If you understand these past questions you should have success with any changes that arise. Tests may consist of several types of questions. We have additional books on each subject should more study be advisable or necessary for you. Finally, the more you study, the better prepared you will be. This book is intended to be the last thing you study before you walk into the examination room. Prior study of relevant texts is also recommended. NLC publishes some of these in our Fundamental Series. Knowledge and good sense are important factors in passing your exam. Good luck also helps. So now study this Passbook, absorb the material contained within and take that knowledge into the examination. Then do your best to pass that exam.

EXAMINATION SECTION

EXAMINATION SECTION
TEST 1

DIRECTIONS: Each question or incomplete statement is followed by several suggested answers or completions. Select the one that BEST answers the question or completes the statement. *PRINT THE LETTER OF THE CORRECT ANSWER IN THE SPACE AT THE RIGHT.*

1. Damage due to electrolysis is USUALLY caused by   1.____

    A. A.C.   B. D.C.
    C. A.C. or D.C.   D. high frequency currents

2. When a current transformer secondary circuit supplies several instruments and relays,   2.____
   as is common practice, the current coils of the

    A. instruments and relays are all connected in parallel
    B. instruments are connected in series and the relays in parallel
    C. relays are connected in series and the instruments in parallel
    D. instruments and relays are all connected in series

3. The SMALLEST number of single-phase A.C. wattmeters required to measure the power   3.____
   in a three-phase, 4-wire, unbalanced A.C. circuit is

    A. 1   B. 2   C. 3   D. 4

4. When connected across a D.C. source of supply, the shunt field coils of a generator take   4.____
   0.15 amperes. A 500 ohm resistor is connected in series with the coils across the same
   source thereby reducing the current to 0.5 amperes. The resistance of the field is _____
   ohms.

    A. 167   B. 250   C. 500   D. 1500

5. If work on any power department equipment is to be performed by more than one crew, a   5.____
   separate Hold-Off must be obtained by each crew.
   However, only one Hold-Off shall be allowed when the equipment is being

    A. cleaned
    B. repaired
    C. taken out of service in an emergency
    D. subjected to a high voltage test

6. If copper weighs 0.32 lbs. per cubic inch, the weight of a 1100 foot coil of #6 bare copper   6.____
   wire, diameter 162.0 mils, is given by the product of 0.785 multiplied by 0.32, multiplied
   by

    A. 0.162 x 0.162 x 12,000   B. 162 x 162 x 12,000
    C. 0.162 x 0.162 x 1000   D. 162 x 162 x 1000

7. A neon test lamp can be used to check   7.____

    A. if a circuit is A.C. or D.C.
    B. the phase rotation of a source of supply
    C. the power factor of a circuit
    D. the polarity markers of a transformer

8. A storage battery has an open circuit voltage of 120 volts. When supplying a load of 50 amperes, the battery voltage drops to 115 volts.
   This indicates that 0.1 ohms is the

   A. combined resistance of the load and battery
   B. equivalent resistance of the external load
   C. internal resistance of the battery
   D. difference between the load resistance the the battery resistance

9. To control a lamp independently from three different locations, you would use _____ switches.

   A. two 3-way and one 4-way
   B. three 3-way
   C. one 3-way and two 4-way
   D. three single pole

10. If a self-excited motor generator fails to build up on the first run, the FIRST thing to do is to

    A. check the armature insulation resistance
    B. reverse the connections to the shunt field
    C. increase the field resistance
    D. decrease the speed of the motor

11. If the specific gravity reading of a lead acid battery is 1.235 at 100° F and the correction factor is 0.0004 per degree Fahrenheit, then the true reading at 80° F is MOST NEARLY

    A. 1.238
    B. 1.243
    C. 1.253
    D. 1.265

12. To sound an alarm when a circuit is broken, you would use a(n) _____ alarm.

    A. open circuit
    B. short circuit
    C. closed circuit
    D. reverse current

13. A systematic layout of work and proper assignment of men, by a foreman, will NOT affect the

    A. kind of supervision needed in the performance of the job
    B. quality of the finished work
    C. time required to do the work
    D. amount of work to be done

14. A single-phase potential of 60 volts is required for test purposes. A 600 volt source and two identical transformers with 600 volt primary windings and 120 volt secondary windings are available.
    To get the required 60 volts, the transformers should be connected with the primaries in _____, secondaries in _____.

    A. parallel; series
    B. series; series
    C. parallel; parallel
    D. series; parallel

15. The insulation resistance of a cable is 50 megohms per 1000 feet between conductor and lead sheath.
    If four 500 foot lengths and one 1000 foot length of this cable were spliced in series to make a feeder, the insulation resistance of this feeder would be NEAREST to _____ megohms.

    A. 17
    B. 75
    C. 100
    D. 250

16. One of your helpers, on the 4:00 P.M. to 12:00 Midnight watch, was injured as a result of slipping on some oil near an oil switch compartment. This oil switch splashed the oil when it opened under overload that morning. It was inspected, cable high-potted, barriers removed, and put back in service at 3:00 P.M.
    The accident to the helper would MOST likely be codified as due to

    A. poor housekeeping
    B. carelessness on the part of the party injured
    C. defective equipment
    D. proper safety appliances not used

17. Undercharging of a lead acid storage battery may cause

    A. buckling of the plates
    B. excessive loss of water
    C. excessive corrosion of terminals
    D. loss of internal resistance

18. If an armature is 7" in diameter and rotates at 1750 RPM, the surface speed, in feet per minute, is NEAREST to

    A. 1,600   B. 3,210   C. 6,420   D. 38,500

19. Knowledge of the *Schedule of Working Conditions For Employees in the Power Department* will be MOST useful to a foreman in dealing with subordinates when

    A. assigning service ratings
    B. delegating responsibility
    C. determining monetary allowances
    D. enforcing safety measures

20. Sparking at the commutator of a D.C. motor is NOT likely to be caused by

    A. a short-circuited armature coil
    B. running below rated speed
    C. vibration of the machine
    D. an open circuited armature coil

21. A D.C. milliammeter may be adapted for A.C. measurements with the use of a(n)

    A. paper condenser   B. instrument shunt
    C. instrument transformer   D. selenium rectifier

22. A foreman of another department complains to you that some of your men did not cooperate fully on a job which was done jointly with his men.
    With respect to this complaint, you should

    A. investigate to substantiate or disprove the charge
    B. ignore the matter because the job is finished
    C. tell the other foreman that your men always cooperate
    D. simply cite instances when his men did not cooperate with you

23. To prevent damage to rigid conduit, bends shall be made on a radius of NOT less than _____ times the internal diameter.

    A. 20 B. 15 C. 10 D. 5

24. A section of D.C. bus consisting of four 6x1/4 inch copper bars is to be removed. The gap is to be bridged using 1,000,000 circular mil cable.
    In order that the current density in the cable shall not exceed that in the bus, the number of cables used should be AT LEAST

    A. 8 B. 7 C. 6 D. 4

25. A simple series circuit consists of a 10 ohm resistor in series with a 5 ohm capacitive reactance and a 5 ohm inductive reactance.
    The impedance of this circuit, in ohms, is

    A. 3.2 B. 10 C. 14.1 D. 20

26. Assume that you have been the foreman in charge of a crew for several weeks when you notice that the men are beginning to show a dislike for you and that this is adversely affecting their morale and efficiency.
    Your BEST procedure is to

    A. loosen up the discipline of the crew
    B. insist on better discipline
    C. take stock of yourself to determine if you are to blame
    D. pay no attention as foremen are bound to be disliked no matter what they do

27. A 6000 watt heater is composed of three similar resistance units connected in delta to a 3-phase, 208 volt supply. The resistance, in ohms, of each resistance unit is MOST NEARLY

    A. 37.4 B. 21.6 C. 12.5 D. 9.5

28. A static capacitor used for power factor correction is connected to the line in _____ with a machine drawing _____ current.

    A. series; leading   B. series; lagging
    C. parallel; leading   D. parallel; lagging

29. In a bar to bar test applied to a D.C. armature, you find that the voltage between two adjacent commutator bars is almost equal to the applied test voltage.
    This is an indication that the armature coil between the two bars is

    A. open B. grounded C. shorted D. reversed

30. The MAIN purpose of the capacitor and auxiliary winding on a capacitor motor is to

    A. provide starting torque
    B. increase the speed
    C. permit reversal of direction of rotation
    D. improve the power factor

31. When thermal overload relays are used for the protection of motors, their primary purpose is to protect the motors in case of

   A. reversal of phases in the supply
   B. low line voltage
   C. sustained overload
   D. short circuit

32. Current transformer secondary circuits are NOT usually fused because

   A. excessive voltage may be developed in the secondary circuit if the fuse blows
   B. the wiring is heavy enough to carry large currents safely
   C. protection is provided by fuses in the primary circuit
   D. the secondary current cannot exceed 5 amperes

33. Time delay would be expected in relays for protection against

   A. short-circuit   B. overspeed
   C. flash-over   D. overload

34. When completing the charging of a lead-acid battery, the charging rate should be lowered to prevent violent gassing. The MAIN reason for this is that

   A. the gases given off are explosive
   B. violent gassing tends to loosen the active material on the positive plates
   C. evaporation of the acid weakens the electrolyte
   D. the cell containers are subjected to excessive gas pressure

35. Assume that an auto transformer has a ratio of 2 to 1. If the primary voltage is 100 volts and the secondary load has a resistance of 5 ohms, the current, in amperes, in the secondary winding is MOST NEARLY

   A. 5   B. 10   C. 15   D. 20

36. A 3-phase, 230 volt motor draws 100 amperes at 90% power factor.
    The power input to this motor is MOST NEARLY _____ kw.

   A. 20.7   B. 35.8   C. 44.2   D. 62.1

37. The purpose of a starting compensator used with a large squirrel cage induction motor is to

   A. increase the starting torque of the motor
   B. reduce the starting current taken from the line
   C. improve the power factor during the starting period
   D. reduce the time required to attain full speed

38. When acquainting a group of newly appointed maintainer helpers with the nature of their duties, it would be LEAST important to include information pertaining to

   A. issuing *Hold-Offs*   B. safety practices
   C. housekeeping procedures   D. lunch periods

39. Upon learning that one of your subordinates went to your superior and, by a misrepresentation of facts, obtained his consent to a request you denied, your BEST course of action would be to

    A. demand that the man be brought up on charges
    B. do nothing to avoid prolonging the incident
    C. explain the situation to your superior
    D. request that the man be transferred

40. The PRINCIPAL reason for slotting commutators of D.C. machines is to

    A. reduce the weight of the commutator
    B. improve the insulation between segments
    C. provide air passages under the brushes for cooling
    D. relieve the commutator of high mica

41. The term *emergency work*, as used in the Schedule of Working Conditions, includes

    A. work made necessary by the failure of another employee to report for duty
    B. any work at a maintainer's level which is performed by a helper
    C. any work which an employee is required to perform outside of his scheduled working hours
    D. overtime work in excess of 4 hours not made necessary by the absence of another employee

42. An induction motor is supplied by a three-phase transformer. The primary of this transformer is connected in delta and the secondary is connected in delta for starting and in wye for running.
    The ratio of the running to the starting voltage is

    A. 0.58   B. 1.41   C. 1.73   D. 2.0

43. A 4-pole, 60-cycle induction motor has a full load slip of 5 percent.
    The full load speed of this motor is _____ RPM.

    A. 1710   B. 1890   C. 3420   D. 3780

44. In order that a circuit breaker may be opened by remote control, it must be equipped with a(n)

    A. inverse time trip   B. instantaneous trip
    C. trip-free mechanism   D. shunt trip

45. The power dissipated in a 50 millivolt, 10,000 ampere shunt of a D.C. panel ammeter when carrying 5,000 amperes is _____ watts.

    A. 100   B. 125   C. 250   D. 500

46. Lead-covered cables in manholes are bonded together and grounded.
    The MAIN reason for this is to

    A. equalize any stray currents which may enter the cable
    B. drain off any current due to a fault in the cable
    C. ground any induced currents flowing in the lead sheath
    D. prevent corrosion of the lead sheath by electrolytic action

47. The high potential test of cables serves PRIMARILY to measure the 47._____
    A. insulation resistance
    B. tensile strength of the insulation
    C. moisture absorption qualities of the insulation
    D. ability of the insulation to withstand operating voltages

48. The sequence of operation of electrical equipment is shown by a(n) 48._____
    A. working drawing   B. detailed drawing
    C. elementary diagram   D. layout diagram

49. A tungsten lamp is sometimes placed across a relay operating coil to give the relay a 49._____
    time delay characteristic. This is possible because the resistance of the filament is
    A. greater cold than when lit
    B. the same cold or lit
    C. determined by the relay resistance
    D. greater when lit than when cold

50. A device used to prevent damage in case the leads are reversed when reconnecting a 50._____
    three-phase motor is a reverse _____ relay.
    A. phase   B. current   C. power   D. voltage

KEY (CORRECT ANSWERS)

1.	B	11.	B	21.	D	31.	C	41.	D
2.	D	12.	C	22.	A	32.	A	42.	C
3.	C	13.	D	23.	C	33.	D	43.	A
4.	B	14.	D	24.	A	34.	B	44.	D
5.	D	15.	A	25.	B	35.	A	45.	B
6.	A	16.	A	26.	C	36.	B	46.	D
7.	A	17.	A	27.	B	37.	B	47.	D
8.	C	18.	B	28.	D	38.	A	48.	C
9.	A	19.	C	29.	A	39.	C	49.	D
10.	B	20.	B	30.	A	40.	D	50.	A

ELECTRICITY
EXAMINATION SECTION
TEST 1

DIRECTIONS: Each question or incomplete statement is followed by several suggested answers or completions. Select the one that BEST answers the question or completes the statement. *PRINT THE LETTER OF THE CORRECT ANSWER IN THE SPACE AT THE RIGHT.*

1. You intend to use type R insulated aluminum wire for a circuit that is to have 75 amps flowing and have 3 wires in a raceway.
   The PROPER size wire to use is #

   A. 4   B. 3   C. 2   D. 1

   1.____

2. An effect caused by dissimilar metals is known as

   A. thermoelectric   B. thermopile
   C. viscosity   D. buoyancy

   2.____

3. Five 5 ohm resistors are connected in parallel across a 2 volt battery.
   The current flowing is _____ amps.

   A. .04   B. .08   C. 2   D. 10

   3.____

4. A 110 volt toaster rated at 550 watts is wound with nichrome wire having a resistance of 1.63 ohms per foot.
   The number of feet of nichrome wire is APPROXIMATELY _____ feet.

   A. 5   B. 13   C. 35   D. 337

   4.____

5. A 0.1 henry inductance operates at 60 cycles.
   The inductive reactance is _____ ohms.

   A. 6   B. 10   C. 18.8   D. 37.7

   5.____

6. The capacity of a 6 mfd condenser connected in series with three 1 mfd condensers in parallel is _____ mfd.

   A. .5   B. 2   C. 6   D. 9

   6.____

7. The D.C. component of the harmonic composition of the output of a full wave rectifier tube is _____ times the peak of the alternating voltage applied to the rectifier.

   A. $1/\pi$ B. $2/\pi$ C. π D. 2π

   7.____

8. A motor is connected to a 2∅ 4 wire circuit. It is drawing 90 amps and is connected with a #1 type R wire.
   The MINIMUM insulation resistance required is _____ ohms.

   A. 10,000   B. 25,000   C. 50,000   D. 500,000

   8.____

9. The MINIMUM size of hard drawn copper wire that may be used for a 500 watt radio transmitter antenna is #

   A. 10   B. 8   C. 6   D. 4

   9.____

10. If you attempted to start a D.C. compound motor in which the series field was open circuited, the motor would

    A. not start
    B. blow a fuse
    C. run away
    D. start in reverse

11. Twenty 15 amp fully loaded 2 wire branch circuits are fed from a balanced 3 wire 1∅ panel.
    The size of type R wire required to feed the panel is

    A. #0   B. #000   C. 250 MCM   D. 500 MCM

12. An air trip free circuit breaker was overheating.
    Of the following, the MOST probable cause is

    A. overload
    B. defective contact points
    C. short circuit
    D. defective pins in the circuit breaker

13. A neon lamp may be used to test for

    A. phase rotation
    B. A.C. or D.C.
    C. power factor
    D. reluctivity of a magnetic circuit

14. 12 lamps in parallel are connected across a 120 volt line. If each lamp takes 0.5 amps and the volt drop of the line is not to exceed 3% of the line voltage, the resistance of each wire supplying the bank of lamps is MOST NEARLY _____ ohms.

    A. 0.3   B. 0.6   C. 2.4   D. 3.6

15. A 3∅ 208 volt system supplies a 3∅ 3 wire delta connected load that draws 100 amps with a .75 P.F.
    The power expended is _____ watts.

    A. 15,600   B. 20,800   C. 27,000   D. 36,000

16. We know that 2 watt-meters will read the power in a balanced 3∅ 3 wire system with unity P.F.

    A. One meter will read zero, the other reads all.
    B. The ratio of the watt-meter readings is less than unity.
    C. The ratio of the watt-meter readings is unity.
    D. The ratio of the watt-meter readings is greater than unity.

17. You would connect the hot wire to a screw shell socket to the

    A. shell
    B. center pin
    C. third terminal
    D. grounded terminal

18. With reference to a selinium rectifier, the LEAST important factor in determining the current output is _____ the stack.

    A. number of cells in
    B. area of each cell in
    C. shape of
    D. spacing of the cells in

19. To change a cumulative motor to a cumulative generator, you would   19._____

    A. reverse the fields
    B. reverse the series field only
    C. reverse the armature and field
    D. shift the rocker arm

20. To reverse a capacitor motor, you would reverse   20._____

    A. both auxiliary and main winding
    B. the line leads
    C. the auxiliary winding
    D. the condenser

21. If the D.C. field of a synchronous motor is overexcited,   21._____

    A. it will run faster
    B. it will run slower
    C. line current will be leading
    D. it will hunt

22. A D.C. shunt generator is operated at normal speed. When the field circuit is opened, a small voltage is generated. When the field circuit is closed, the voltage generated is smaller.   22._____
You should

    A. clean the brushes
    B. increase the speed
    C. reverse the armature and field
    D. reverse rotation

23. When replacing a D.C. blowout coil, it is MOST important to   23._____

    A. have its resistance the same as the old coil
    B. have its resistance higher than the old coil
    C. see that the magnetic field reacts
    D. install it when the contacts are open

24. The secondary leads between the controller and resistor of a heavy intermittent duty wound rotor motor shall be in percentage of full load secondary current AT LEAST   24._____

    A. 45%   B. 65%   C. 85%   D. 110%

25. In selecting a reversing type motor starter for maximum protection, you would choose one that is   25._____

    A. separately controlled
    B. mechanically and electrically interlocked
    C. electrically interlocked
    D. mechanically interlocked

4 (#1)

KEY (CORRECT ANSWERS)

1. C   11. B
2. A   12. B
3. C   13. B
4. B   14. A
5. D   15. C

6. B   16. C
7. B   17. B
8. C   18. B
9. A   19. B
10. A   20. C

21. C
22. D
23. D
24. C
25. B

TEST 2

DIRECTIONS: Each question or incomplete statement is followed by several suggested answers or completions. Select the one that BEST answers the question or completes the statement. *PRINT THE LETTER OF THE CORRECT ANSWER IN THE SPACE AT THE RIGHT.*

1. To start an induction motor with a wound rotor under load, you would use 1.____

   A. a compensator
   B. resistance in the rotor circuit
   C. a 3 point starting box
   D. a 4 point starting box

2. A 500 KW load with 0.7 P.F. is fed by a 3 wire 208 volt line. The line current is MOST NEARLY _____ amps. 2.____

   A. 1390   B. 1984   C. 3434   D. 5418

3. The synchronous speed of a 4 pole 25 cycle A.C. motor is 3.____

   A. 750 RPM   B. 375 RPM   C. 3750 RPM   D. not fixed

4. In a D.C. time delay system using a capacitor and a resistor, capacitor farads represented by C, ohm resistor represented by R, time constant T in seconds should be represented by 4.____

   A. RC   B. 1/RC   C. R/C   D. C/R

5. 3-1ø transfers have the primary rated at 2300 volts and the secondary winding rated at 208 volts. 5.____
   How much the transformers be connected to a 4000 volt primary line to obtain a secondary line voltage of 208 volts?

   A. $\Delta - \Delta$ B. $\Delta - Y$ C. $Y - \Delta$ D. $Y - Y$

6. A transformer has 2 secondary windings. When connected in parallel, the voltage of the secondary is 115 volts. When connected in series with a neutral center tap, the voltage is 230/115 volts. 6.____
   What is the ratio of the current when the windings are connected in parallel to the current of the windings in series?

   A. 1/3   B. 1/2   C. Twice   D. Same

7. What current should a feeder be capable of carrying to supply motors rated 40 amps, 20 amps, 20 amps, and 10 amps? _____ amps. 7.____

   A. 90   B. 100   C. 125   D. 170

8. 3 way and 4 way switches are connected 8.____

   A. on circuits less than 5 amps   B. across the line
   C. in series with the line   D. to the neutral

13

9. Some thyratron controlled resistance welders employ a circuit in which two tubes are connected *back to back* so that each tube carries current on alternate half-cycles. This type of connection is also called
    A. inverse-parallel connection
    B. push-pull connection
    C. tank circuit
    D. Hartley circuit

10. The EMF of a generator is 115 volts and has an internal resistance of 0.02 ohms. The terminal voltage is _____ volts.
    A. 100
    B. 112.7
    C. 115
    D. 120

11. A D.C. series hoist motor employs resistance shunted across the armature for fast stopping when the line is disconnected. The method is known as
    A. magnetic braking
    B. counter EMF braking
    C. dynamic braking
    D. plugging

12. When rigid conduit enters a box, you would use
    A. locknuts and connectors
    B. locknuts
    C. locknuts and bushings
    D. connectors

13. A 3∅ 25 H.P. 208 volt motor with .8 P.F. and 90% efficiency takes _____ amps.
    A. 65
    B. 72
    C. 89
    D. 125

14. Electricians solder is made of tin and lead. The proportion of tin to lead is
    A. 50/50
    B. 60/40
    C. 70/30
    D. hard core solder

15. In a 2∅ 3 wire circuit, the outside leg to neutral voltage is 100 volts. The voltage between the outside legs is _____ volts.
    A. 100
    B. 141
    C. 173
    D. 200

16. In pulling in 4 #10 type R wires and 2 #12 type R wires in a rewiring job, the conduit fill may be _____%.
    A. 31
    B. 40
    C. 50
    D. 60

17. A 3 volt battery having 0.2 ohms internal resistance is connected in parallel with a 1.5 volt battery having an internal resistance of 0.1 ohm. The circulating current will be _____ amps.
    A. 5
    B. 10
    C. 15
    D. 20

18. A 20 H.P. 3∅ 220 volt wound rotor induction motor takes a full load current of _____ amps.
    A. 38
    B. 52
    C. 57
    D. 64

19. How many circuits would a 3 wire 1Ø panel have to supply 40 200 watt lamps, 6 appliance circuits, and 2 spare circuits?

   A. 8   B. 12   C. 15   D. 20

20. For boxes not over 100 cubic inches, the sheet steel shall be _____ gauge.

   A. 10   B. 14   C. 18   D. 20

21. A hospital operating room is to be supplied with 120 volts D.C. There is 120 volt D.C. with a grounded neutral available.
   To obtain D.C. without a grounded neutral, you would use a

   A. rectifier   B. converter
   C. motor generator   D. transformer

22. Collector wires for a crane are supported at 25 foot intervals.
   The MINIMUM wire size that may be used is #

   A. 2   B. 4   C. 6   D. 8

23. A branch circuit feed for a crane motor that runs through a room where the temperature exceeds 167°F (75°C) shall be type

   A. R   B. SB   C. AF   D. fire retardant

24. The MINIMUM size equipment grounding conductor for high tension vertical distribution transformer cases is #

   A. 10   B. 4   C. 00   D. 0000

25. A 3Ø wound rotor induction motor is tested by starting it and allowing it to come up to speed with the load removed. The motor starts and reaches its normal no-load speed satisfactorily, then its speed suddenly drops to about one-half of the normal no-load speed.
   The MOST probable cause is

   A. one of the rotor leads opens due to centrifugal force
   B. a pair of poles becomes shorted, thereby reducing the speed
   C. the motor resistance becomes shorted, thereby reducing the speed
   D. one of the rotor leads touches another rotor lead due to centrifugal force

KEY (CORRECT ANSWERS)

1. B
2. B
3. A
4. A
5. C

6. C
7. B
8. C
9. A
10. C

11. C
12. C
13. B
14. A
15. B

16. C
17. A
18. B
19. C
20. B

21. C
22. C
23. B
24. D
25. A

TEST 3

DIRECTIONS: Each question or incomplete statement is followed by several suggested answers or completions. Select the one that BEST answers the question or completes the statement. *PRINT THE LETTER OF THE CORRECT ANSWER IN THE SPACE AT THE RIGHT.*

1. Two characteristics of a synchronous motor are

   A. adjustable power factor and adjustable speed
   B. constant power factor and constant speed
   C. adjustable power factor and constant speed
   D. adjustable speed and constant speed

2. The MAXIMUM voltage to ground for elevator control pushbuttons is _____ volts.

   A. 120   B. 208   C. 300   D. 600

3. The MINIMUM size equipment grounding conductor for high tension vertical distribution transformer cases is #

   A. 10   B. 8   C. 000   D. 0000

4. Vertical conduits for high tension steel armored cable shall be supported by building construction at intervals not exceeding _____ feet and encased in _____ inches of concrete.

   A. 25; 2   B. 35; 2   C. 35; 3   D. 25; 3

5. The MINIMUM distance that shall be maintained between bare metal parts having a potential difference of 125 volts on panelboards is

   A. 3/4"   B. 1"   C. 1 1/4"   D. 1 1/2"

6. The frequency of the current at a load, as compared to that of the generator

   A. depends on the load   B. is lower
   C. is higher   D. is the same

7. The resistance to the flow of magnetic flux is known as

   A. permanence   B. reluctance
   C. resistance   D. reactance

8. A conductor cutting magnetic lines of force at the rate of 10^8 lines per second will generate

   A. 1 ohm   B. 1 ampere   C. 1 watt   D. 1 volt

9. A 30 25 H.P., 208 volt motor with .8 P.F. and 90% efficiency takes a full load current of APPROXIMATELY _____ amperes.

   A. 65   B. 72   C. 89   D. 125

10. Which of the following relays is the MOST commonly used relay for industrial use?

    A. Overcurrent   B. Phase
    C. Reverse current D. Split-phase

11. If you reversed the line leads to a D.C. compound motor, it would

    A. stop
    B. reverse
    C. run in the same direction
    D. slow down

12. A D.C. generator has an EMF of 115 volts and an internal resistance of .07 ohms. What is the voltage at the load when it is delivering 50 amperes?

    A. 111.5   B. 115   C. 118.5   D. 120

13. The sockets allowed for a 500 watt incandescent lamp is

    A. candelabra   B. intermediate   C. medium   D. mogul

14. A single circuit may be used to feed several small motors providing the largest motor does NOT exceed _____ amps.

    A. 6   B. 10   C. 15   D. 20

15. A D.C. shunt generator with commutating poles has the brushes set in the correct neutral position. However, when load is applied to this machine, violent sparking occurs at the brushes.
    The MOST likely trouble is that the

    A. speed is too low
    B. shunt field connections are reversed
    C. interpole connections are reversed
    D. armature reaction is short-circuited

16. If a D.C. shunt wound generator fails to build up, the one of the following conditions which is MOST likely to be the cause is

    A. improper brush pressure
    B. there may be too much residual magnetism in the machine
    C. the field resistance may be lower than the critical field resistance
    D. the field resistance may be greater than the critical field resistance

17. In a certain installation, thermal cutouts in the controller are used for motor running protection. In addition, enclosed fuses are installed at the point where the motor conductors are connected to the feeder.
    The purpose of these fuses is to

    A. limit the motor current to 115% of rating
    B. protect the conductors against short circuits
    C. protect the conductors against sustained overload
    D. protect the motor against any overload

18. A compensator is a device used with induction motors to

    A. compensate for electrical losses of the motor
    B. compensate for the voltage drop in motor circuit
    C. increase the starting torque of the motor
    D. decrease the line voltage at starting

19. The difference between the operating speed and the synchronous speed of an induction machine is called the   19.____

   A. slip   B. phase   C. accelerating   D. frequency

20. An A.C. magnetic clutch draws 5 amperes from a 120 volt, 60 cycle line. If the power consumed is 300 watts, the power factor is   20.____

   A. 0.5   B. 0.6   C. 0.7   D. 0.8

21. The condenser in a single-phase capacitor motor is connected   21.____

   A. in series with the starting winding
   B. in series with the motor terminals
   C. permanently across the motor terminals
   D. in parallel with the starting winding

22. The MOST important reason for not fusing the neutral in a 3 wire 120/240 volt system is because   22.____

   A. it is rarely overloaded
   B. the additional protection is unnecessary
   C. the blowing of a neutral fuse may unbalance the voltages
   D. it would blow only on a short circuit

23. The MINIMUM distance that shall be maintained between bare metal parts having a potential difference of 120 volts and being mounted on the same panelboard surface is _____ inch(es).   23.____

   A. 3/4   B. 1   C. 1 1/4   D. 1 1/2

24. When the current in an outside leg of a balanced 2 phase 3 wire system is 150 amps, the neutral current is _____ amps.   24.____

   A. 0   B. 141   C. 173   D. 211

25. You would fuse a 2 phase 3 wire system   25.____

   A. in the neutral   B. in all three wires
   C. in one outside wire   D. in both outside wires

KEY (CORRECT ANSWERS)

1. C
2. C
3. D
4. A
5. A

6. B
7. B
8. D
9. B
10. C

11. C
12. A
13. D
14. A
15. C

16. D
17. B
18. D
19. A
20. A

21. A
22. C
23. A
24. D
25. D

TEST 4

DIRECTIONS: Each question or incomplete statement is followed by several suggested answers or completions. Select the one that BEST answers the question or completes the statement. *PRINT THE LETTER OF THE CORRECT ANSWER IN THE SPACE AT THE RIGHT.*

1. To be installed properly, a single-throw knife switch should be mounted so that   1.____

    A. gravity tends to close it
    B. it is in a vertical position
    C. it is accessible only to qualified persons
    D. gravity tends to open it

2. The SMALLEST electrical trade size conduit used for wiring work is the _____ inch.   2.____

    A. 1/2   B. 3/8   C. 3/4   D. 1

3. When the starter for a 220 volt, direct-current, shunt motor, whose full-load armature current is 20 amperes, is in the first contact position, the total resistance in the armature circuit, to permit the motor to start with 110% of rated torque, should be APPROXIMATELY _____ ohms.   3.____

    A. 7.3   B. 10   C. 11   D. 22

4. A junction box is used for the purpose of running through six No. 12 type R wires and for joining four other No. 12 type R wires.   4.____
The SMALLEST size junction box that should be used is

    A. 1 1/2 inch x 3 1/4 inch octagonal
    B. 1 1/2 inch x 4 inch square
    C. 1 1/2 inch x 4 11/16 inch square
    D. 2 1/8 inch x 4 11/16 inch square

5. A number of 115-volt, 30 watt, A.C. fluorescent lamps are installed in a plant which has a 3-phase, 4-wire service (208-volt power and 120-volt lighting). When large motor loads come on the system, the lamps flicker and at times may even go out.   5.____
Of the following, the MOST probable cause of the trouble is that

    A. the lamps are poorly designed for 60 cycle frequency
    B. all or part of the choke is shorted
    C. the voltage drops below critical operating value
    D. the lamps are defective

6. Ninety 100-watt, 120 volt lamps are connected to a 3-phase, 3-wire, 120-volt feeder.   6.____
The current in each wire for a balanced load is APPROXIMATELY _____ amperes.

    A. 25   B. 33   C. 43   D. 75

7. If a motor has a circuit breaker of the time limit type for overload protection, its setting, at most, shall be _____% of name plate current rating of motor.   7.____

    A. 110   B. 115   C. 125   D. 130

21

2 (#4)

8. In a three wire attachment plug, _____ terminal(s) must be identified.   8.___
   A. all   B. one   C. two   D. no

9. As a general rule, a fuse or circuit breaker should be provided at every point where   9.___
   A. the load current increases
   B. a change is made in the size of wire
   C. the load current decreases
   D. the circuit is connected to variable load

10. In accordance with the New York City Electrical Code, surgical operating and auxiliary rooms shall be classified as Class _____ hazardous locations.   10.___
    A. I   B. II   C. III   D. IV

11. A circuit contains two one-henry inductance coils in parallel and two one-henry inductance coils in series. Assuming that the magnetic field of one inductor cannot act upon the turns of another, then the TOTAL inductance of this combination is _____ H.   11.___
    A. 4   B. 3 1/2   C. 2 1/2   D. 1/4

12. The thickness of the insulation of #14 R wire should be not less than   12.___
    A. 2/64"   B. 3/64"   C. 4/64"   D. 5/64"

13. Twenty 15 amp full loaded 2 wire branch circuits are fed from a balanced 3 wire 10 panel.   13.___
    The size type R wire required to feed the panel is #
    A. 00   B. 000   C. 250 MCM   D. 500 MCM

14. A D.C. motor takes a full load current of 50 amperes.   14.___
    A thermal cutout protecting the motor against overloads should be set to open the circuit for not more than _____ amps.
    A. 60   B. 62.5   C. 75   D. 100

15. The correct type branch circuit fuse to use for a 28.7 amp, 7 1/2 H.P., 230 volt, D.C., 1750 R.P.M., 90% efficient motor is a _____ type.   15.___
    A. cartridge ferrule   B. cartridge knife blade
    C. plug fuse   D. hexagonal tamper-resistant

16. The MAXIMUM setting for the running protection of 20 H.P., 220 volt 3-phase motor is _____ amps.   16.___
    A. 65   B. 70   C. 75   D. 80

17. A single phase load connected to a 220 volt line takes 30 amps and dissipates 5,280 watts.   17.___
    The power factor is
    A. 50%   B. 60%   C. 70%   D. 80%

18. A 3-phase motor takes 48 amps at 230 volts. 18._____
    If the P.F. is 85%, the power is MOST NEARLY _____ watts.

    A. 9,380   B. 11,000   C. 14,500   D. 16,230

19. A 3∅ 208-volt system supplies a 3-wire delta connected load that takes 100 amps with a 19._____
    75% P.F.
    The power expended is _____ watts.

    A. 15,600   B. 20,800   C. 27,000   D. 36,000

20. A 500 KW load with 0.7 P.F. is fed by a 3∅ 3-wire, 208-volt line. 20._____
    The line current is MOST NEARLY _____ amps.

    A. 1390   B. 1984   C. 3434   D. 5418

21. The current of a 60 cycle, 1∅ A.C. magnetic clutch that consumes 360 watts and oper- 21._____
    ates on 120 volts with a 60% P.F. is _____ amps.

    A. 3   B. 5   C. 8   D. 11

22. A circuit breaker of the current limiting type used for overload protection on a 20 amp 22._____
    D.C. motor should be set no greater than _____ amps.

    A. 20   B. 23   C. 25   D. 30

23. A 3-wire, 2-phase system is 100 volts per phase. 23._____
    The voltage between the outside legs will be _____ volts.

    A. 100   B. 141   C. 173   D. 200

24. Vertical conduits for high tension steel armored cable shall be supported by building con- 24._____
    struction at intervals not exceeding _____ feet and shall be encased in at least _____
    inches of concrete.

    A. 25; 2   B. 35; 2   C. 35; 3   D. 25; 3

25. A round bus bar has a 250000 CMA. 25._____
    What is the area of the bar in square inches?

    A. .1   B. .2   C. .4   D. .8

KEY (CORRECT ANSWERS)

1.	D	11.	C
2.	A	12.	A
3.	B	13.	B
4.	C	14.	B
5.	C	15.	A
6.	C	16.	A
7.	C	17.	D
8.	B	18.	D
9.	B	19.	C
10.	A	20.	B

21. B
22. C
23. B
24. A
25. B

———

TEST 5

DIRECTIONS: Each question or incomplete statement is followed by several suggested answers or completions. Select the one that BEST answers the question or completes the statement. *PRINT THE LETTER OF THE CORRECT ANSWER IN THE SPACE AT THE RIGHT.*

1. The circuit resistance of three 2 ohm resistance connected in series is _____ ohm(s).   1._____
   A. 2/3 B. 1 C. 2 D. 6

2. Five 2 ohm resistors are connected in series across a 10 volt battery. The current flowing in the circuit is _____ amp(s).   2._____
   A. .1 B. 1 C. .5 D. 5

3. The circuit resistance of a 5 ohm resistor connected in parallel with a 45 ohm resistor is _____ ohms.   3._____
   A. 5.0 B. 4.5 C. .2 D. .02

4.   4._____

   The overall resistance of the above circuit is _____ ohms.
   A. 13 B. 16 C. 20 D. 30

5. The TOTAL capacity of three 1 mfd condensers in series is _____ mfd.   5._____
   A. 1/3 B. 1 C. 1 1/3 D. 3

6. The capacity of a circuit of three 1 mfd condensers in parallel is _____ mfd.   6._____
   A. 1/3 B. 1 C. 1 1/3 D. 3

7. A circuit contains two one-henry inductance coils in parallel and two one-henry inductance coils in series. Assuming that the magnetic field of one inductor cannot act upon the terms of the other, then the TOTAL inductance of this combination is _____ henrys.   7._____
   A. 4 B. 3 1/2 C. 2 1/2 D. 1/4

8. A 2-wire circuit feeds a 90 amp 27 H.P. motor from a 220 volt D.C. panel 300 feet away. The resistance of the wire is 0.1532 ohms per 1000 feet. The voltage at the load is MOST NEARLY _____ volts.   8._____
   A. 212 B. 205 C. 216 D. 200

9. A 2-wire 35 amp 225 volt load is fed from a 230 volt panel. The resistance of one of the wires is _____ ohms.   9._____
   A. 0.071 B. 0.143 C. 0.657 D. 6.57

25

10. The capacity of a 6 mfd condenser connected in series with three 1 mfd condensers in parallel is _____ mfd.

    A. 0.5   B. 2   C. 6   D. 9

11. The total inductance in henrys of 4 induction coils of 1 henry each connected in parallel is _____ H.

    A. 1 1/4   B. 1/4   C. 4   D. 1

12. A bank of 12 lamps are connected in parallel across a 120 volt line.
    If each lamp takes 0.5 amps and the volt-drop of the line is not to exceed 3% of the line voltage, the resistance of each wire supplying the bank of lamps is MOST NEARLY _____ ohms.

    A. 0.3   B. 0.6   C. 2.4   D. 3.6

13. An insulated wire carries a marking of RH-10.
    The wire is

    A. #10 heater cord
    B. #10 wire for 600 volt use only
    C. for 30 circuits only
    D. suitable for 1000 volt use

14. The type of wire that may be used for switchboard wiring only is

    A. TW   B. TA   C. R   D. AVA

15. A wire that has a maximum operating temperature of 140°F is type

    A. R   B. RH   C. V   D. TA

16. Four #10 and two #12 wires may be installed in the same conduit when rewiring with thinner conductors if the sum of the cross-sectional areas of the individual wires is NOT more than

    A. 40%   B. 60%   C. 50%   D. 43%

17. The total resistance of a circuit containing one 1 ohm resistor in series with a combination of three 1 ohm resistors in parallel is _____ ohm(s).

    A. 1/4   B. 4   C. 1 1/3   D. 3

18. The allowable current carrying capacity of conductors in a raceway or cable

    A. is independent of the number of conductors
    B. shall be reduced to 70% of table values if more than three conductors are contained in the raceway or cable
    C. shall be reduced to 50% of the table values if more than six conductors are contained in the raceway or cable
    D. shall be reduced to 80% for four to six conductors and to 70% for seven to 24 conductors within the same raceway or cable

19. A conductor of 19 strands, each having a diameter of 0.0664 inch has a capacity of one amp for each 500 C.M.A. The current capacity is _____ amps.

    A. 256.3   B. 333   C. 2.5   D. 167.5

20. The conductor having the HIGHEST current capacity is

    A. asbestos insulated
    B. rubber insulated
    C. varnish cambric insulated
    D. lead covered

21. Number 4 aluminum TW conductor is to be used in wiring a certain job. The rated current capacity of this wire is _____ amps.

    A. 55   B. 50   C. 65   D. 70

22. Three aluminum type R wires are installed in a conduit to carry 75 amperes. The SMALLEST size that may be used is #

    A. 4   B. 3   C. 2   D. 1

23. A circuit breaker is said to be trip-free if

    A. its bearings are free acting
    B. it will not remain closed under overload
    C. it operates through a current
    D. used on D.C. only

24. For a feeder over 200 feet long, you would use

    A. higher voltage
    B. larger fuses
    C. smaller wire than the original
    D. larger wire than the original

25. A wire that has a MAXIMUM operating temperature of 167°F is type

    A. R   B. RH   C. TW   D. RHH

KEY (CORRECT ANSWERS)

1.	D	11.	B
2.	B	12.	B
3.	B	13.	D
4.	C	14.	B
5.	A	15.	A
6.	D	16.	C
7.	C	17.	C
8.	A	18.	D
9.	A	19.	D
10.	B	20.	A

21. A
22. C
23. B
24. D
25. B

TEST 6

DIRECTIONS: Each question or incomplete statement is followed by several suggested answers or completions. Select the one that BEST answers the question or completes the statement. *PRINT THE LETTER OF THE CORRECT ANSWER IN THE SPACE AT THE RIGHT.*

1. The rating of a cartridge enclosed fuse with a green label is 1.____

    A. 15 amps or less at 250 volts
    B. over 15 amps at 250 volts
    C. 15 amps at 600 volts
    D. over 18 amps at 600 volts

2. If a motor has a circuit breaker of the time-limit type for overload protection, its setting, at most, shall be set no higher of full load than 2.____

    A. 110%   B. 115%   C. 125%   D. 130%

3. An air circuit breaker calibrated at 15 amps should be constructed so that the calibration can be changed 3.____

    A. easily done   B. with difficulty
    C. impossible   D. not done

4. A fuse or circuit breaker should be provided at every point where 4.____

    A. the load current increases
    B. a change is made in the size of wire
    C. load current decreases
    D. the circuit is connected to variable load

5. How many amps should a feeder conductor be capable of carrying if it is to supply motors, each rated respectively, at 40 amps, 20 amps, 20 amps, and 10 amps? 5.____

    A. 90   B. 100   C. 125   D. 170

6. A 15 amp, 125 volt circuit may protect several small motors providing 6.____

    A. the largest motor is less than 1 HP
    B. the disconnecting switch is in the same location
    C. the largest motor draws no more than 6 amps
    D. they are within sight of the controller

7. On a heavy starting duty wound rotor motor, the secondary resistor leads shall have a current capacity of AT LEAST 7.____

    A. 35%   B. 45%   C. 85%   D. 110%

8. Plug fuses having a hexagonal-shaped window have a MAXIMUM rating of _____ amps. 8.____

    A. 10   B. 15   C. 20   D. 30

29

9. In a certain installation, thermal cutouts in the controller are used for motor running protection. In addition, enclosed fuses are installed at the point where the motor conductors are connected to the feeder.
   The purpose of these fuses is to

   A. limit the motor current to 115% of rating
   B. protect the conductors against sustained overload
   C. protect the conductors and motor against short circuits
   D. protect the motor against any overload

10. An automatic overload circuit breaker will protect the equipment in the circuit when its overload device is

    A. in parallel with the conductors supplying the load
    B. rated in watts
    C. in parallel with other circuit breakers
    D. in series with the conductors supplying the load

11. A cartridge fuse with a blue label has a rating of _____ amps at _____ volts.

    A. 15; 125   B. 15; 250   C. 30; 250   D. 15; 600

12. To select the proper fuse, it is necessary to know the

    A. amperes *only*
    B. volts *only*
    C. watts *only*
    D. amperes and volts

13. A silver sand fuse is

    A. not approved
    B. approved up to 600 amps
    C. approved in all sizes
    D. used with circuit breakers only

14. Plug fuses and cartridge fuses in casings for use with screw shell useholders have a rating no more than _____ amps.

    A. 0-15   B. 0-20   C. 0-30   D. 0-60

15. A D.C. shunt generator with commutating poles has the brushes set in the correct neutral position. However, when load is applied to this machine, violent sparking occurs at the brushes.
    The MOST likely trouble is that the

    A. speed is too low
    B. shunt field connections are reversed
    C. interpole connections are reversed
    D. armature reaction is short-circuited

16. If a D.C. shunt wound generator fails to build up, the one of the following conditions which is MOST likely to be the cause is

    A. improper brush pressure
    B. there may be too much residual magnetism in the machine
    C. the field resistance may be lower than the critical field resistance
    D. the field resistance may be greater than the critical field resistance

17. A D.C. shunt generator is operated at normal speed. When the field circuit is opened, a small voltage is generated. When the field circuit is closed, the voltage generated is smaller.
    You should

    A. clean the brushes
    B. increase the speed
    C. decrease the field rheostat
    D. reverse rotation

18. To change a cumulative motor to a cumulative generator, you would

    A. reverse the fields
    B. reverse the series field *only*
    C. reverse the armature and field
    D. shift the rocker arm

19. A certain differential compound motor has a tendency to start in the wrong direction. The one of the following procedures which will PROPERLY cure this defect is

    A. short the shunt field on starting
    B. open the shunt field on starting
    C. short the series field on starting
    D. reverse the shunt field connections

20. A 3 point and a 4 point starting box have no-voltage protection.
    Sometimes a 3 point starting box is used because

    A. it costs less
    B. the wiring is simpler
    C. it also has no-field protection
    D. it also has no-voltage release

21. The field of a D.C. series motor should be

    A. wound with wire of sufficient cross-section to carry the armature current
    B. connected in parallel with the armature
    C. wound with small, high resistance wire
    D. wound with a non-inductive winding

22. Excessive sparking at the brushes of a D.C. crane motor is NOT caused by

    A. low mica
    B. reversed interpoles
    C. an open armature winding
    D. sticking brushes

23. The armature of a 220 volt shunt motor takes 20 amps at full load. It supplies 110% torque for starting.
    The resistance at the first point on the starting box is _____ ohms.

    A. 7.5   B. 10   C. 11   D. 22

24. The CORRECT way to remove wire insulation is to
    A. use a knife at an angle to the wire
    B. ring the insulation with a knife and pull off
    C. crush the insulation with pliers and pull off
    D. break the insulation with a hammer and pull off

25. A growler is used to test for
    A. a shorted armature
    B. motor noises
    C. a grounded field
    D. a grounded armature

KEY (CORRECT ANSWERS)

1. B
2. C
3. D
4. B
5. B

6. C
7. B
8. B
9. C
10. D

11. B
12. D
13. C
14. C
15. C

16. D
17. D
18. B
19. C
20. D

21. A
22. A
23. B
24. A
25. A

EXAMINATION SECTION
TEST 1

DIRECTIONS: Each question or incomplete statement is followed by several suggested answers or completions. Select the one that BEST answers the question or completes the statement. PRINT THE LETTER OF THE CORRECT ANSWER IN THE SPACE AT THE RIGHT.

1. That system of electric braking in which the traction motors are used as generators and the kinetic energy of the load is used as the actuating means for exerting a retarding force is known as _____ braking.

    A. track B. magnetic C. dynamic D. generator

2. Thermal overload protective devices used for motor running protection protect the motor against

    A. a short-circuit
    B. overcurrent at starting
    C. transient overloads
    D. normal operating overloads

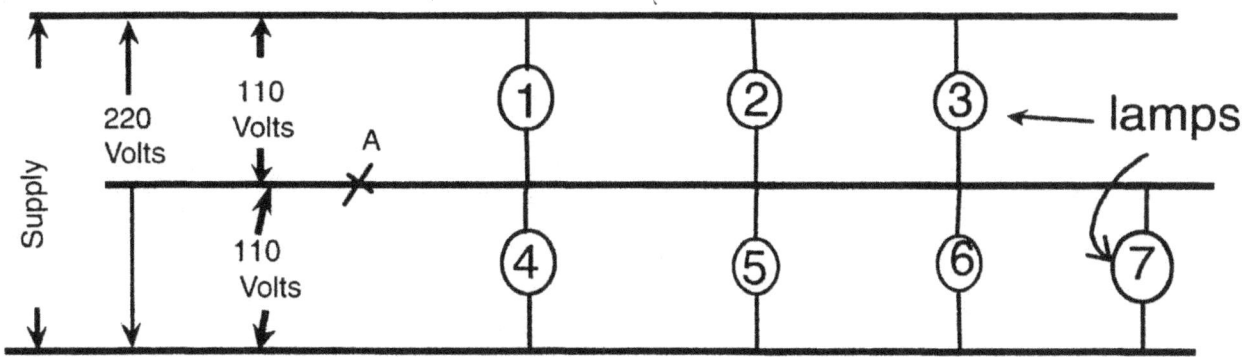

3. In the above diagram, the center conductor breaks at point A.

    A. Lamps 1, 2, and 3 will burn with greater brilliancy than lamps 4, 5, 6 and 7.
    B. Lamps 1, 2, and 3 will burn dimmer than lamps 4, 5, 6, and 7.
    C. All lamps will be extinguished.
    D. All lamps will burn with the same brilliancy that they had before the center lead opened.

4. In ordering standard cartridge fuses it is necessary to specify ONLY the

    A. current capacity
    B. voltage of the circuit
    C. current capacity and the voltage of the circuit
    D. power to be dissipated

5. The current input per phase under rated-load conditions for a 200-H.P., 3 phase, 2300-volt, 0.8 P. F., induction motor which is 90% efficient is _____ amperes.

    A. 52 B. 90 C. 41.6 D. 46.8

6. Referring to problem 5 above, the power input under rated-load conditions is APPROXIMATELY

    A. 149 K.W. B. 96 K.W. C. 166 K.W. D. 332 K.W.

7. Three single-phase transformers are connected in delta on both the primary and secondary sides.
   If one of the transformers burns out the system can continue to operate but its capacity, in terms of the capacity of the original arrangement, is reduced to

   A. 66 2/3%   B. 57.8%   C. 115%   D. 100%

8. In order to successfully operate two compound-wound d.c. generators in parallel it is necessary to use

   A. a compensating winding   B. an equalizer connection
   C. a series field diverter   D. commutating poles

9. If a given machine requires a full-load torque of 30 pound-feet and runs at a speed of 1800 R.P.M., the size of direct-coupled motor required to drive this machine is APPROXIMATELY _____ H.P.

   A. 10.3   B. 20.6   C. 15.3   D. 5.2

10. Oil is used in many large transformers to

    A. lubricate the core   B. lubricate the coils
    C. insulate the coils   D. insulate the core

11. A certain machine is driven by a 1750-R.P.M. d.c. shunt motor. If the power supply is to be changed to three-phase, 60 cycles, a.c., the MOST suitable replacement motor would be a _____ motor.

    A. series   B. repulsion
    C. squirrel-cage induction D. capacitor

12. Two transformers with ratios of 1.2 are to be connected in parallel. To test for proper connections the circuit of the above diagram is used.
    The transformers may be connected in parallel by connecting lead a to lead b if the voltmeter shown reads _____ volts.

    A. 120   B. 240   C. zero   D. 480

13. You were asked to calculate the electric bill for the last month. The kilowatt-hour meter reads 99,010 K.W.-hrs. at the end of the previous month and now reads 00,110 K.W.-hrs. The demand meter reads 75 K.W.
    The energy rate is:
    For the first 500 K.W.-hrs. $0.04 per K.W.-hr.
    For the next 300 K.W.-hrs. $0.03 per K.W.-hr.
    For the next 200 K.W.-hrs. $0.02 per K.W.-hr.
    For all in excess of 100 K.W.-hrs. $0.01 per K.W.-hr.
    The demand rate is $0.50 per K.W.
    The total electric bill is

    A. $71.50   B. $67.50   C. $83.50   D. $74.50

13.____

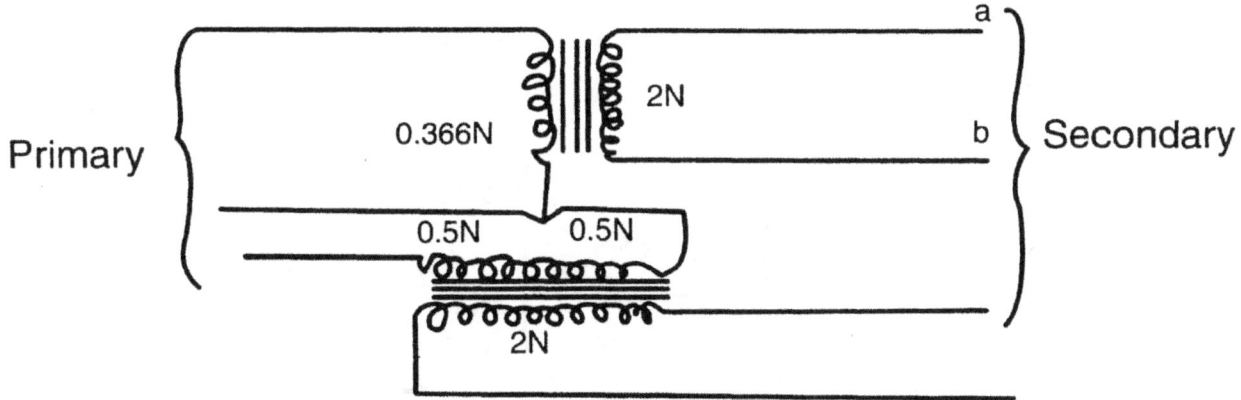

14. If the primary leads in the above diagram are connected to a three-phase, three-wire, 208 volt system and the transformation ratios are as indicated on the diagram, the secondary leads will form a _____ -phase, _____ -wire system.

    A. three   four
    B. two   four
    C. four   five
    D. three   three

14.____

15. In the circuit of the above diagram, the voltage between the secondary leads a and b is _____ volts.

    A. 208   B. 120   C. 416   D. 240

15.____

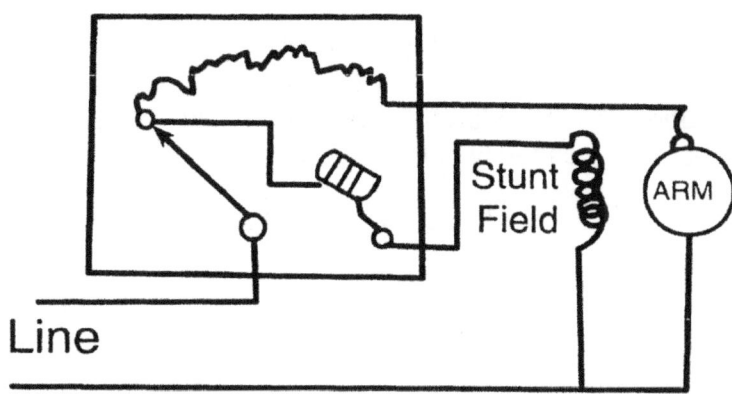

16. The circuit of the above diagram shows a d.c. motor starter. One of the features of this starting box is a(n) _____ release.

    A. overload   B. no-field   C. reverse-current   D. underload

17. For starting a three-phase induction motor a three-phase transformer is used with its primaries connected in delta and its secondaries connected in delta for starting and in wye for running.
    The ratio of the running to the starting voltage is

    A. 3 : 1   B. 2 : 1   C. 1.73 : 1   D. 1.41 : 1

18. A booster transformer is a transformer connected

    A. in such a manner as to increase the load on the line by a fixed percentage
    B. as a delta-connected bank
    C. as an auto-transformer to raise the line voltage by a fixed percentage
    D. in such a manner as to raise the frequency by a fixed percentage

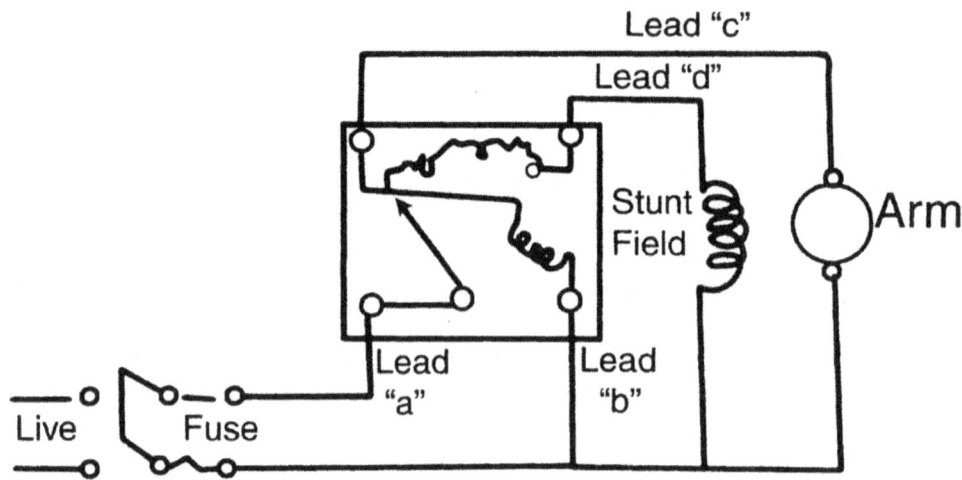

19. The motor shown in the above figure does not operate correctly. When the line switch is closed the fuses blow.
    To correct this fault leads _____ and _____ should be interchanged.

    A. leads *a* and *b*
    B. leads *a* and *c*
    C. leads *b* and *d*
    D. leads *c* and *d*

20. A standard stranded cable contains 19 strands. When measured with a micrometer the diameter of each strand is found to be 105.5 mils.
    If, under certain conditions, the allowable current density is 600 C.M. per ampere the allowable current-carrying capacity of this conductor is _____ amperes.

    A. 236   B. 176.3   C. 352.5   D. 705

21. For MAXIMUM safety the magnetic contactors used for reversing the direction of rotation of a motor should be

    A. electrically interlocked
    B. electrically and mechanically interlocked
    C. mechanically interlocked
    D. operated from independent sources

22. When the starter for a 250-volt, direct-current shunt motor whose full-load armature current is 20 amperes, is in the first contact postion, the total resistance in the armature circuit, to permit the motor to start with 150% of rated torque, should be APPROXIMATELY _____ ohms.

    A. 5 B. 8 C. 12 D. 20

23. If the allowable current density for copper bus bars is 1000 amperes per square inch, the current-carrying capacity of a circular copper bar having a diameter of two inches is APPROXIMATELY _____ amperes.

    A. 1050 B. 2320 C. 3140 D. 4260

24. A rotary converter, operating at unity power factor, may be made to take a leading power factor by

    A. *increasing* the d.c. field strength of the machine
    B. *decreasing* the d.c. field strength of the machine
    C. *decreasing* the speed at which it operates
    D. *increasing* the speed at which it operates

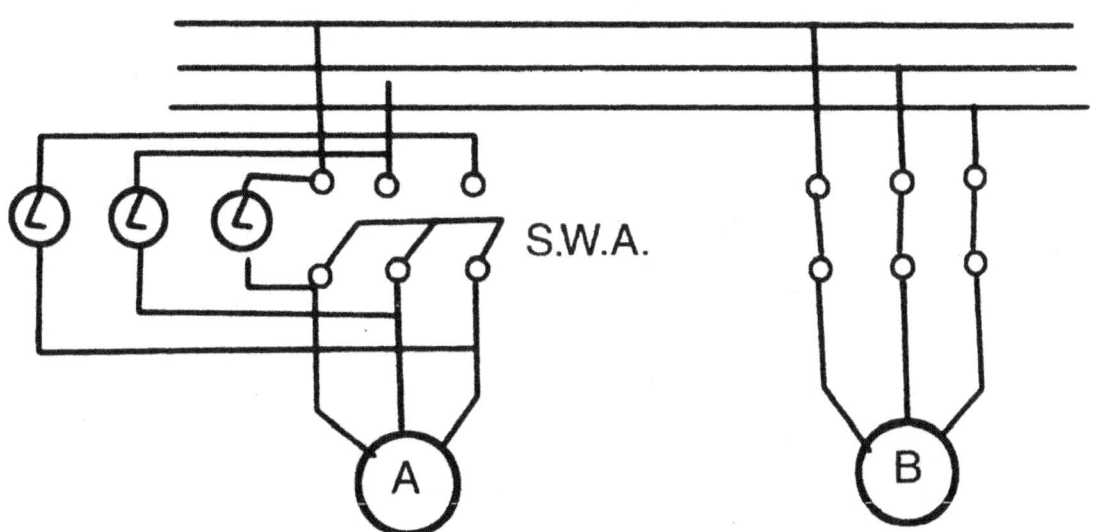

25. Two alternators are to be synchronized for parallel operation, the correct synchronization being indicated by three lamps, as shown in the above diagram.
    The CORRECT time to close switch A is

    A. when the lamps are at maximum brilliancy
    B. when the lamps are dark
    C. just before the lamps reach maximum brilliancy
    D. just after the lamps reach maximum brilliancy

26. The maximum voltage-drop between a d.c. motor and switchboard is not to exceed one percent of the supply voltage.
If the supply voltage is 200 volts, the full-load current of the motor 100 amperes, the distance from the switchboard to the motor 100 feet, and the resistivity of copper 10 ohms per C.M.-foot, the size wire required in C.M. is

   A. 25,000   B. 50,000   C. 100,000   D. 200,000

27. One foot of a certain size of nichrome wire has a resistance of 1.63 ohms.
To make a heating element for a toaster that will use 5 amperes at 110 volts, the number of feet of wire needed is APPROXIMATELY

   A. 17.9   B. 8.2   C. 5.5   D. 13.5

28. A tri-free circuit breaker is one that

   A. is tripped from a shunt-circuit through a relay
   B. can be tripped only by an operator
   C. cannot be tripped when the operating lever is held in the closed position
   D. can be tripped by the overload mechanism even though the operating lever is held in the closed position

29. The following equipment is required for a 2-*line return-call* electric bell circuit: 2 bells, 2 metallic lines,

   A. 2 ordinary push-buttons, and one set of batteries
   B. 2 return-call push-buttons and 2 sets of batteries
   C. 2 return-call push-buttons and one set of batteries
   D. one ordinary push-button, one return-call push button and one set of batteries

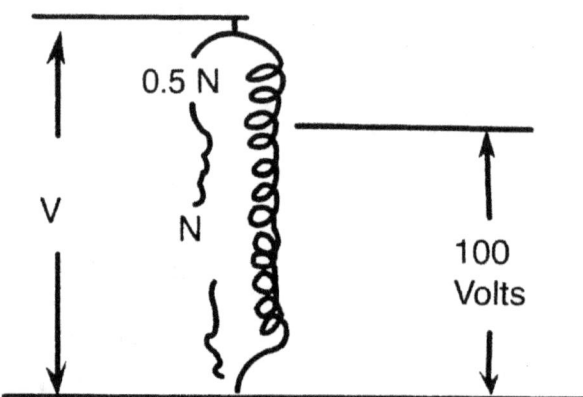

30. An auto-transformer with turns ratio as indicated in the above sketch is connected to a 100-volt, 60-cycle supply on the low-tension side.
The voltage, V, on the high tension side is _____ volts.

   A. 50   B. 100   C. 150   D. 200

31. The MINIMUM size of grounding conductor for a direct or alternating-current system is

   A. No. 14   B. No. 10   C. No. 8   D. No. 6

32. The thickness of insulation for a No. 8 rubber-covered conductor for use at NOT more than 2000 volts shall be _____ of an inch.

    A. 2/64ths   B. 3/64ths   C. 4/64ths   D. 5/64ths

33. A gutter whose width is 36 inches shall be constructed of sheet metal of thickness NOT less than No. _____ U.S. standard sheet metal gauge.

    A. 10   B. 12   C. 14   D. 16

34. The MAXIMUM voltage permitted on the push buttons of elevator signalling circuits shall be _____ volts to ground.

    A. 300   B. 125   C. 250   D. 600

35. Electric motors installed in hospital operating rooms shall be of the _____ proof type.

    A. water   B. explosion   C. dust   D. light

36. Connecting batteries in parallel instead of in series _____ of the batteries.

    A. *increases* the current output
    B. *decreases* the life
    C. *increases* the voltage
    D. *decreases* the current output

37. To charge a storage battery, one would use

    A. either a.c. or d.c.   B. a.c. only
    C. d.c. only   D. only low frequency a.c.

38. A transformer is USUALLY used to

    A. change a.c. to d.c.
    B. raise or lower a.c. voltage
    C. change d.c. to a.c.
    D. change the frequency of the a.c. supply

39. The commutator of a d.c. generator

    A. keeps the current flowing in one direction in the load circuit
    B. reverses the current direction in the armature
    C. acts only as a sliding electrical contact
    D. changes a.c. to d.c. within the armature

40. The number of fresh dry cells that should be connected in series to obtain 12 volts is

    A. 2   B. 6   C. 8   D. 12

KEY (CORRECT ANSWERS)

1.	C	11.	C	21.	B	31.	C
2.	D	12.	C	22.	B	32.	D
3.	A	13.	A	23.	C	33.	A
4.	C	14.	B	24.	A	34.	A
5.	A	15.	C	25.	B	35.	B
6.	C	16.	B	26.	C	36.	A
7.	B	17.	C	27.	D	37.	C
8.	B	18.	C	28.	D	38.	B
9.	A	19.	D	29.	B	39.	A
10.	C	20.	C	30.	C	40.	C

TEST 2

DIRECTIONS: Each question or incomplete statement is followed by several suggested answers or completions. Select the one that *BEST* answers the question or completes the statement. *PRINT THE LETTER OF THE CORRECT ANSWER IN THE SPACE AT THE RIGHT.*

1. Of the following, the BEST conductor of electricity is 1.____

   A. tungsten B. iron C. aluminum D. carbon

2. A 600-volt cartridge fuse is MOST readily distinguished from a 250-volt cartridge fuse of the same ampere rating by comparing the 2.____

   A. insulating materials used B. shape of the ends
   C. diameters D. lengths

3. Many power-transformer cases are filled with oil. The purpose of the oil is to 3.____

   A. prevent rusting of the core
   B. reduce a.c. hum
   C. insulate the coils from the case
   D. transmit heat from the coils and core

4. In order to make certain that a 600-volt circuit is dead before working on it, the BEST procedure is to 4.____

   A. test with a voltmeter
   B. *short* the circuit quickly with a piece of insulated wire
   C. see if any of the insulated conductors are warm
   D. disconnect one of the wires of the circuit near the feed

5. When closing an exposed knife switch on a panel, the action should be positive and rapid because there is less likelihood of 5.____

   A. the operator receiving a shock
   B. the operator being burned
   C. the fuse blowing
   D. injury to equipment connected to the circuit

6. Lubrication is never used on 6.____

   A. a knife switch
   B. a die when threading conduit
   C. wires being pulled into a conduit
   D. a commutator

7. If one plug fuse in a 110-volt circuit blows because of a short-circuit, a 110-volt lamp screwed into the fuse socket will 7.____

   A. burn dimly B. remain dark C. burn out D. burn normally

8. Of the following, the LEAST undesirable practice if a specified wire size is not available for part of a circuit is to 8.____

A. use two wires of 1/2 capacity in parallel as a substitute
B. use the next larger size wire
C. use a smaller size wire if the length is short
D. reduce the size of the fuse and use smaller wire

9. If it is necessary to increase slightly the tension of an ordinary coiled spring in a relay, the PROPER procedure is to

A. cut off one or two turns
B. compress it slightly
C. stretch it slightly
D. unhook one end, twist and replace

10. As compared with solid wire, stranded wire of the same gage size is

A. given a higher current rating
B. easier to skin
C. larger in total diameter
D. better for high voltage

11. Motor frames are USUALLY positively grounded by a special connection in order to

A. remove static
B. protect against lightening
C. provide a neutral
D. protect against shock

12. If a live conductor is contacted accidentally, the severity of the electrical shock is determined PRIMARILY by

A. the size of the conductor
B. whether the current is a.c. or d.c.
C. the contact resistance
D. the current in the conductor

13. If a snap switch rated at 5 amperes is used for an electric heater which draws 10 amperes, the MOST likely result is that the

A. circuit fuse will be blown
B. circuit wiring will become hot
C. heater output will be halved
D. switch contacts will become hot

14. To straighten a long length of wire which has been tightly coiled, before pulling it into a conduit run, a good method is to

A. roll the wire into a coil in the opposite direction
B. fasten one end to the floor and whip it against the floor from the other end
C. draw it over a convenient edge
D. hold the wire at one end and twist it with the pliers from the other end

15. The wire size MOST commonly used for branch circuits in residences is

A. #14   B. #16   C. #12   D. #18

16. If the applied voltage on an incandescent lamp is increased 10%, the lamp will

A. have a longer life
B. burn more brightly
C. consume less power
D. fail by insulation breakdown

17. You would expect that the overload trip coil on an ordinary air circuit breaker would have 17._____

    A. heavy wire
    B. fine wire
    C. many turns
    D. heavily insulated wire

18. A cycle counter is an electrical timer which, when energized by alternating current, counts the number of cycles until it is de-energized. 18._____
    If a cycle counter is energized from a 60-cycle power supply for ten seconds, the reading of the instrument should be

    A. 6   B. 10   C. 60   D. 600

19. The MOST practical way to determine in the field if a large coil of #14 wire has the required length for a given job is to 19._____

    A. weigh the coil
    B. measure one turn and count the turns
    C. unroll it into another coil
    D. make a visual comparison with a full coil

20. A frequency meter is constructed as a potential device, that is, to be connected across the line. 20._____
    A logical reason for this is that

    A. only the line voltage has frequency
    B. a transformer may then be used with it
    C. the reading will be independent of the varying current
    D. it is safer than a series device

21. It is usually not safe to connect 110 volts d.c. to a magnet coil designed for 110 volts a.c. because the 21._____

    A. insulation is insufficient
    B. iron may overheat
    C. wire may overheat
    D. inductance may be too high

22. The MOST satisfactory temporary replacement for a 40-watt, 120-volt incandescent lamp, if an identical replacement is not available, is a lamp rated at _____ watts, _____ volts. 22._____

    A. 100; 240   B. 60; 130   C. 40; 32   D. 15; 120

23. If the following bare copper wire sizes were arranged in the order of increasing weight per 1000 feet, the CORRECT arrangement would be 23._____

    A. #00, #40, #8
    B. #40, #00, #8
    C. #00, #8, #40
    D. #40, #8, #00

24. The purpose of having a rheostat in the field circuit of a d.c. shunt motor is to 24._____

    A. control the speed of the motor
    B. minimize the starting current
    C. limit the field current to a safe value
    D. reduce sparking at the brushes

25. The resistance of a 1000-ft. length of a certain size copper wire is required to be 10.0 ohms ± 2%.
    This wire would NOT be acceptable if the resistance was _____ ohms.

    A. 10.12   B. 10.02   C. 10.22   D. 9.82

26. The LEAST important action in making a good soldered connection between two wires is to

    A. use the proper flux   B. clean the wires well
    C. use plenty of solder   D. use sufficient heat

27. Of the following, the BEST conductor of electricity is

    A. aluminum   B. carbon   C. copper   D. water

28. Good practice requires that the end of a piece of conduit be reamed after it has been cut to length.
    The purpose of the reaming is to

    A. prevent insulation damage when pulling in the wires
    B. finish the conduit accurately to length
    C. make the threading easier
    D. remove loose rust

29. According to the national electrical code, a run of conduit between two outlet boxes should not contain more than four quarter bends.
    The MOST likely reason for this limitation is that more bends will

    A. result in cracking the conduit
    B. make the pulling of the wire too difficult
    C. increase the wire length unnecessarily
    D. not be possible in one standard length of conduit

30. Asbestos is commonly used as the covering of electric wires in locations where there is likely to be high

    A. voltage   B. temperature   C. humidity   D. current

31. Portable lamp cord is LIKELY to have

    A. steel armor   B. stranded wires
    C. paper insulation   D. number 8 wire

32. The one of the following terms which could NOT correctly be used in describing a knife switch is

    A. quick-break   B. single throw   C. four-pole   D. toggle

33. With respect to common electric light bulbs, it is CORRECT to state that the

    A. circuit voltage has no effect on the life of the bulb
    B. filament is made of carbon
    C. base has a left hand thread
    D. lower wattage bulb has the higher resistance

34. The resistance of a 1000-foot coil of a certain size copper wire is 10 ohms. If 300 feet are cut off, the resistance of the remainder of the coil is _____ ohms.

    A. 7   B. 3   C. 0.7   D. 0.3

35. The term *15 ampere* is COMMONLY used in identifying a(n)

    A. insulator   B. fuse   C. conduit   D. outlet box

36. When connecting the two lead wires of a test instrument to a live d.c. circuit, the BEST procedure is to first make the negative or ground connection and then the positive connection.
    The reason for this procedure is that

    A. electricity flows from positive to negative
    B. there is less danger of accidental shock
    C. the reverse procedure may blow the fuse
    D. less arcing will occur when the connection is made

37. To make a good soldered connection between two stranded wires, it is LEAST important to

    A. twist the wires together before soldering
    B. use enough heat to make the solder flow freely
    C. clean the wires carefully
    D. apply solder to each strand before twisting the two wires together

38. When a step-up transformer is used, it increases the

    A. voltage   B. current   C. power   D. frequency

39. Lock nuts are frequently used in making electrical connections on terminal boards.
    The purpose of such lock nuts is to

    A. make tighter connections with less effort
    B. make it difficult to tamper with the connections
    C. avoid stripping the threads
    D. keep the connections from loosening through vibration

40. The core of an electro-magnet is USUALLY

    A. aluminum   B. lead   C. brass   D. iron

41. A stranded wire is given the same size designation as a solid wire if it has the same

    A. cross-sectional area   B. weight per foot
    C. overall diameter   D. strength

42. One advantage of cutting 1" rigid conduit with a hacksaw rather than a 3-wheel pipe cutter is that

    A. the cut can be made with less exertion
    B. the pipe is not squeezed out of round
    C. less reaming is required after the cut
    D. no vise is needed

43. Assume that the field leads of a large, completely disconnected d.c. motor are not tagged or otherwise marked. You could readily tell the shunt field leads from the series field leads by the

    A. length of the leads
    B. size of wire
    C. thickness of insulation
    D. type of insulation

44. Standard electrician's pliers should NOT be used to

    A. bend thin sheet metal
    B. crush insulation on wires to be skinned
    C. cut off nail points sticking through a board
    D. hold a wire in position for soldering

45. The device used to change a.c. to d.c. is a

    A. frequency   B. regulator   C. transformer   D. rectifier

46. The CHIEF advantage of using stranded rather than solid conductors for electrical wiring is that stranded conductors are

    A. more flexible
    B. easier to skin
    C. smaller
    D. stronger

47. One identifying feature of a squirrel-cage induction motor is that it has no

    A. windings on the stationary part
    B. commutator or slip rings
    C. air gap
    D. iron core in the rotating part

48. If a cartridge fuse is hot to the touch when you remove it to do some maintenance on the circuit, this MOST probably indicates that the

    A. voltage of the circuit is too high
    B. fuse clips do not make good contact
    C. equipment on the circuit starts and stops frequently
    D. fuse is oversize for the circuit

49. The instrument MOST commonly used to determine the state of charge of a lead-acid storage battery is the

    A. thermometer
    B. hydrometer
    C. voltmeter
    D. ammeter

50. Rigid conduit must be installed as to prevent the collection of water in it between outlets. In order to meet this requirement, the conduit should NOT have a

    A. low point between successive outlets
    B. high point between successive outlets
    C. low point at an outlet
    D. high point at an outlet

KEY (CORRECT ANSWERS)

1. C	11. D	21. C	31. B	41. A
2. D	12. C	22. B	32. D	42. C
3. D	13. D	23. D	33. D	43. B
4. A	14. B	24. A	34. A	44. C
5. B	15. A	25. C	35. B	45. D
6. D	16. C	26. C	36. B	46. A
7. D	17. A	27. C	37. D	47. B
8. B	18. D	28. A	38. A	48. B
9. A	19. B	29. B	39. D	49. B
10. C	20. C	30. B	40. D	50. A

TEST 3

DIRECTIONS: Each question or incomplete statement is followed by several suggested answers or completions. Select the one that BEST answers the question or completes the statement. PRINT THE LETTER OF THE CORRECT ANSWER IN THE SPACE AT THE RIGHT.

1. When a test lamp is connected to the two ends of a cartridge fuse on an operating switchboard, the indication in ALL cases will be that this fuse is

   A. blown if the test lamp remains dark
   B. good if the test lamp lights
   C. blown if the test lamp lights
   D. good if the test lamp remains dark

2. If one copper wire has a diameter of 0.128 inch, and another copper wire has a diameter of 0.064 inch, the resistance of 1,000 feet of the first wire compared to the same length of the second wire is

   A. one half   B. one quarter   C. double   D. four times

3. If the allowable current in a copper bus bar is 1,000 amperes per square inch of cross-section, the width of a standard 1/4" bus bar designed to carry 1500 amperes would be

   A. 2"   B. 4"   C. 6"   D. 8"

4. It is not possible to obtain a 200-watt light-bulb that is as small in all dimensions as the standard 150-watt light-bulb.
   The PRINCIPAL advantage to users resulting from this reduction in size is that

   A. maintenance electricians can carry many more light-bulbs
   B. two sizes of light-bulbs can be kept in the same storage space
   C. the higher wattage bulb can now fit into certain lighting fixtures
   D. less breakage is apt to occur in handling

5. A carbon brush in a d.c. motor should exert a pressure of about 1 1/2 lbs. per square inch on the commutator.
   A much lighter pressure would be MOST likely to result in

   A. sparking at the commutator
   B. vibration of the armature
   C. the brush getting out of line
   D. excessive wear of the brush holder

6. The number of watts of heat given off by a resistor is expressed by the formula I^2R.
   If 10 volts is applied to a 5-ohm resistor, the heat given off will be _____ watts.

   A. 500   B. 250   C. 50   D. 20

7. When a number of rubber insulated wires are being pulled into a run of conduit having several sharp bends between the two pull boxes, the pulling is likely to be hard and the wires are subjected to considerable strain.
   For these reasons it is ADVISABLE in such a case to

A. push the wires into the feed end of the conduit at the same time that pulling is being done
B. pull in only one wire at a time
C. use extra heavy grease
D. pull the wires back a few inches after each forward pull to gain momentum

8. The plug of a portable tool should be removed from the convenience outlet by grasping the plug and not by pulling on the cord because

   A. the plug is easier to grip than the cord
   B. pulling on the cord may allow the plug to fall on the floor and break
   C. pulling on the cord may break the wires off the plug terminals
   D. the plug is generally better insulated than the cord

9. When using a pipe wrench, the hand should be placed so as to pull instead of push on the wrench.
The basis for this recommendation is that there is less likelihood of

   A. the wrench slipping
   B. injury to the hand if the wrench slips
   C. injury to the pipe if the wrench slips
   D. stripped pipe threads

10. High voltage switches in power plants are commonly so constructed that their contacts are submerged in oil.
The purpose of the oil is to

    A. help quench arcing
    B. lubricate the contacts
    C. cool the switch mechanism
    D. insulate the contacts from the switch framework

11. In a storage battery installation consisting of twenty 2-volt cells connected in series, a leak develops in one of the cells and all the electrolyte runs out of it.
The terminal voltage across the twenty cells will now be

    A. 40   B. 38   C. 2   D. 0

12. When removing the insulation from a wire before making a splice, care should be taken to avoid nicking the wire MAINLY because then the

    A. current carrying capacity will be reduced
    B. resistance will be increased
    C. insulation will be harder to remove
    D. wire is more likely to break

13. Good practice dictates that an adjustable open-end wrench should be used PRIMARILY when the

    A. nut to be turned is soft and must not be scored
    B. proper size of fixed wrench is not available
    C. extra leverage is needed
    D. location is cramped permitting only a small turning angle

14. It would generally be poor practice to use ordinary slip-joint pliers to

    A. pull a small nail B. bend a wire
    C. remove a cotter pin D. tighten a machine bolt

15. The a.c. motor which has exactly the same speed at full-load as at no load is the _____ motor.

    A. synchronous B. repulsion C. induction D. condenser

16. A metal bushing is usually screwed on to the end of rigid conduit inside of a junction box. The bushing serves to

    A. center the wires in the conduit
    B. separate the wires where they leave the conduit
    C. protect the wires against abrasion
    D. prevent sagging of the conduit

17. The PROPER abrasive for cleaning the commutator of a d.c. generator is

    A. steel wool B. emery cloth C. sand paper D. soapstone

18. If a *live* 120-volt d.c. lighting circuit is connected to the 120-volt winding of an otherwise disconnected power transformer, the result will be

    A. blowing of the d.c. circuit fuse
    B. magnetization of the transformer fuse
    C. sparking at the transformer secondary terminals
    D. burning out of lights on the d.c. circuit

19. Threaded joints in rigid conduit runs are made watertight through the use

    A. petroleum jelly B. solder C. red lead D. paraffin wax

20. The letters S.P.S.T. frequently found on wiring plans refer to a type of

    A. cable B. switch C. fuse D. motor

21. Renewable fuses differ from ordinary fuses in that

    A. they can carry higher overloads
    B. burned out fuses can be located more easily
    C. burned out fuse elements can be readily replaced
    D. they can be used on higher voltages

22. After No. 10 A.W.G., the next SMALLER copper wire size in common use is No.

    A. 8 B. 9 C. 11 D. 12

23. The BEST of the following tools to use for cutting off a piece of single-conductor #6 rubber insulated lead covered cable is

    A. pair of electrician's pliers B. hacksaw
    C. hammer and cold chisel D. lead knife

24. Toggle bolts are MOST appropriate for use to fasten conduit clamps to a 24.____

　　A. steel column　　　　　　　　B. concrete wall
　　C. hollow tile wall　　　　　　　D. brick wall

25. If a 10-24 by 3/4" machine screw is not available, the screw which could be MOST easily 25.____
modified to use in an emergency is a

　　A. 10-24 by 1/2"　　　　　　　　B. 12-24 by 3/4"
　　C. 10-24 by 1 1/2"　　　　　　　D. 8-24 by 3/4"

26. A standard pipe thread differs from a standard screw thread in that the pipe thread 26.____

　　A. is tapered
　　B. is deeper
　　C. requires no lubrication when cutting
　　D. has the same pitch for any diameter of pipe

27. The material which is LEAST likely to be found in use as the outer covering of rubber 27.____
insulated wires or cables is

　　A. cotton　　　　　　　　　　　B. varnished cambric
　　C. lead　　　　　　　　　　　　D. neoprene

28. In measuring to determine the size of a stranded insulated conductor, the proper place to 28.____
use the wire gauge is on

　　A. the insulation　　　　　　　　B. the outer covering
　　C. the stranded conductor　　　　D. one strand of the conductor

29. Rubber insulation on an electrical conductor would MOST quickly be damaged by continuous contact with 29.____

　　A. acid　　　　B. water　　　　C. oil　　　　D. alkali

30. If a fuse clip becomes hot under normal circuit load, the MOST probable cause is that the 30.____

　　A. clip makes poor contact with the fuse ferrule
　　B. circuit wires are too small
　　C. current rating of the fuse is too high
　　D. voltage rating of the fuse is too low

31. If the input ot a 10 to 1 step-down transformer is 15 amperes at 2400 volts, the secondary output would be NEAREST to _____ amperes at _____ volts. 31.____

　　A. 1.5; 24,000　　B. 150; 240　　C. 1.5; 240　　D. 150; 24,000

32. The resistance of a copper wire to the flow of electricity 32.____

　　A. *increases* as the diameter of the wire increases
　　B. *decreases* as the diameter of the wire decreases
　　C. *decreases* as the length of the wire increases
　　D. *increases* as the length of the wire increases

33. Where galvanized steel conduit is used, the PRIMARY purpose of the galvanizing is to

    A. increase mechanical strength
    B. retard rusting
    C. provide a good surface for painting
    D. provide good electrical contact for grounding

34. The CORRECT method of measuring the power taken by an a.c electric motor is to use a

    A. wattmeter
    B. voltmeter and an ammeter
    C. power factor meter
    D. tachometer

35. Checking a piece of rigid electrical conduit with a steel scale, you measure the inside diameter as 1 1/16" and the outside diameter as 1 5/16".
    The NOMINAL size of this conduit is

    A. 3/4"   B. 1"   C. 1 1/4"   D. 1 1/2"

36. Of the following, it would be MOST difficult to solder a copper wire to a metal plate made of

    A. copper   B. brass   C. iron   D. tin

37. After a piece of rigid conduit has been cut to length, it is MOST important to

    A. ream the inside edge to prevent injury to wires
    B. file the end flat to make an accurate fit
    C. coat the cut surface with red lead to prevent rust
    D. rile the outside edge to a taper for ease in threading

38. Rigid conduit is generally secured to sheet metal outlet boxes by means of

    A. threadless couplings
    B. box connectors
    C. locknuts and bushings
    D. conduit clamps

39. While a certain d.c. shunt motor is driving a light load, part of the field winding becomes short circuited,
    The motor will MOST likely

    A. increase its speed
    B. decrease its speed
    C. remain at the same speed
    D. come to a stop

40. Each time a certain electric heater is turned on, the incandescent lights connected to the same branch circuit become dimmer and when the heater is turned off the lamps become brighter.
    The factor which probably contributes MOST to this effect is the

    A. voltage of the circuit
    B. size of the circuit fuse
    C. current taken by the lamps
    D. size of the circuit conductors

41. Comparing the shunt field winding with the series field winding of a compound d.c. motor, it would be CORRECT to say that the shunt field winding has _____ resistance,

    A. *more* turns but the *lower*
    B. *more* turns and the *higher*
    C. *fewer* turns and the *lower*
    D. *fewer* turns but the *higher*

42. The most important reason for using a fuse-puller when removing a cartridge fuse from the fuse clips is to

    A. prevent blowing of the fuse
    B. prevent injury to the fuse element
    C. reduce the chances of personal injury
    D. reduce arcing at the fuse clips

43. A coil of wire wound on an iron core draws exactly 5 amperes when connected across the terminals of a ten-volt storage battery.
    If this coil is now connected across the ten-volt secondary terminals of an ordinary power transformer, the current drawn will be

    A. *less* than 5 amperes
    B. *more* than 5 amperes
    C. *exactly* 5 amperes
    D. more or less than 5 amperes depending on the frequency

44. A revolution counter applied to the end of a rotating shaft reads 100 when a stop-watch is started. It reads 850 when the stop-watch indicates 90 seconds.
    The average RPM of the shaft is

    A. 8.4   B. 9.4   C. 500   D. 567

45. Motor speeds are generally measured directly in RPM by the use of a

    A. potentiometer   B. manometer   C. dynamometer   D. tachometer

46. To reverse the direction of rotation of a 3-phase motor, it is necessary to

    A. increase the resistance of the rotor circuit
    B. interchange any two of the three line connections
    C. interchange all three line connections
    D. reverse the polarity of the rotor circuit

47. Mica is commonly used in electrical construction for

    A. commutator bar separators   B. switchboard panels
    C. strain insulators   D. heater cord insulation

48. The rating term *1000 ohms, 10 watts* would generally be applied to a

    A. heater   B. relay   C. resistor   D. transformer

49. According to the National Electrical Code, the identified (or grounded) conductor of the branch circuit supplying an incandescent lamp socket must be connected to the screw shell.
    The MOST likely reason for this requirement is that

    A. longer lamp life results
    B. the wiring will be kept more nearly uniform
    C. persons are more likely to come in contact with the shell
    D. the shell can carry heavier currents

50. In an installation used to charge a storage battery from a motor-generator you would LEAST expect to find a(n)
    A. rectifier   B. rheostat   C. voltmeter   D. ammeter

KEY (CORRECT ANSWERS)

1. C	11. D	21. C	31. B	41. B
2. B	12. D	22. D	32. D	42. C
3. C	13. B	23. B	33. B	43. A
4. C	14. D	24. C	34. A	44. C
5. A	15. A	25. C	35. B	45. D
6. D	16. C	26. A	36. C	46. B
7. A	17. C	27. B	37. A	47. A
8. C	18. A	28. D	38. C	48. C
9. B	19. C	29. C	39. A	49. C
10. A	20. B	30. A	40. D	50. A

EXAMINATION SECTION
TEST 1

DIRECTIONS: Each question or incomplete statement is followed by several suggested answers or completions. Select the one that BEST answers the question or completes the statement. *PRINT THE LETTER OF THE CORRECT ANSWER IN THE SPACE AT THE RIGHT.*

1. A 2" conduit is bent 90, with a radius of 1'0" as shown in the sketch at the right. The length of the arc L is MOST NEARLY

    A. 1'0"
    B. 1'7"
    C. 2'0"
    D. 3'2"

    1._____

2. When connecting the leads of a lamp bank to the third rail, a maintainer should make sure the power is

    A. on and then connect either lead first
    B. off and then connect either lead first.
    C. on and then connect the negative lead before connecting the positive lead
    D. off and then connect the positive lead before connecting the negative lead

    2._____

3. In an electrical distribution system, a switch that can carry rated load continuously but cannot interrupt full-load current without damaging the switch is called a(n) _____ switch.

    A. isolating
    C. load interrupting
    B. bolted pressure
    D. horsepower rated safety

    3._____

4. A 100-watt lamp installed in a 110-volt circuit should draw APPROXIMATELY _____ amps.

    A. 0.11   B. 0.91   C. 1.10   D. 2.00

    4._____

5. The symbol shown at the right appearing on a wiring diagram represents a

    A. compound motor
    B. rheostat
    C. trip coil
    D. single-pole switch

    5._____

6. Two-pole circuit breakers are used instead of single-pole circuit breakers to protect 208-volt A.C. lighting circuits because

    A. an overload would not trip a single-pole breaker
    B. a short to ground may not be protected by a single-pole breaker

    6._____

55

C. a line-to-line short would not trip a single-pole circuit breaker
D. if one pole does not function, the other will still protect the circuit

7. Standard conduit for electrical work is supplied in standard lengths of _____ feet.

   A. 20   B. 15   C. 10   D. 5

8. Of the following substances, the one that should be applied to the threads of electrical conduits to waterproof joints is

   A. linseed oil   B. cotton thread
   C. soft solder   D. red lead

9. In accordance with accepted procedures, bends in rigid conduit should be made with a radius of NOT LESS THAN _____ diameter of the conduit.

   A. the   B. 2 times the
   C. 4 times the   D. 10 times the

10. On straight runs, the length of conduit between any two junction boxes should NOT exceed _____ feet.

    A. 10   B. 50   C. 80   D. 150

11. Conduit fastened to concrete in the subway should have supporting clamps separated by a distance NOT to exceed _____ feet.

    A. 5   B. 7   C. 8   D. 10

12. A Ramset tool should be used to drive studs into which of the following surfaces?

    A. Brick   B. Cast iron
    C. Concrete   D. Glazed tile

13. A Ramset tool is in firing position when the tool is lined up with the work surfaces at an angle of

    A. 30°   B. 45°   C. 60°   D. 90°

14. In an incandescent lighting system, the point from which branch currents radiate to all parts of the system is called the

    A. continuous current point
    B. center of distribution
    C. star connection point
    D. terminal center

15. A step-down voltage transformer has a turns ratio of 1.5. If the primary voltage is 440 volts A.C., the secondary voltage is _____ volts.

    A. 5   B. 88   C. 440   D. 2,200

16. In the subway system, the normal B.C. supply for station lighting is _____ volts.

    A. 600   B. 220   C. 208   D. 120

17. A 37.5KVA, single-phase transformer is used to supply a 10KW resistive load. The transformer primary voltage is 120 volts.
    If the secondary voltage is 520 volts, the current drawn by the transformer on the 120-volt side should be APPROXIMATELY _____ amps.

    A. 312   B. 162   C. 83   D. 19

18. Wire having a resistance of 400 ohms per 1,000 feet is to be used for a heater requiring a total resistance of 6 ohms.
    The APPROXIMATE length of wire required is _____ feet.

    A. 15   B. 24   C. 48   D. 67

19. Whenever possible, the direction in which a maintainer should install a run of conduit is from

    A. right to left
    B. left to right
    C. either direction towards the center
    D. the center outward in both directions

20. The wiring insulation best suited for rewiring in existing conduits, where conduit space is limited, is type

    A. TW   B. RH   C. RHW   D. TWN

21. The type of conduit that is recommended for wet locations is

    A. rigid galvanized conduit
    B. E.M.T.
    C. Greenfield
    D. wiremold

22. The current in the neutral wire of a balanced three-phase circuit should be equal to

    A. 2 times the value of the phase current
    B. 1.73 times the value of the phase current
    C. the phase current
    D. zero

23. A dielectric is defined as any non-conducting medium.
    Of the following, the one which should NOT be considered a dielectric is

    A. air   B. water   C. glass   D. ebonite

24. The type of transformer in which the primary and secondary currents flow through the same winding is called a(n) _____ transformer.

    A. auto-   B. insulating
    C. variable ratio   D. constant-current

25. A single-pole lighting switch installed in a single-phase circuit has _____ live wires and _____ neutral wire.

    A. 2; 1   B. 2; no   C. 1; 1   D. 1; no

26. A standard size fuse commonly used for 120-volt lighting circuits is rated as _____ amps.

    A. 60 B. 40 C. 15 D. 5

27. Motor overload protection is commonly provided by heater elements set at _____ of rated motor current.

    A. 125% B. 150% C. 200% D. 225%

28. Of the following safety switch sizes, the one that is NOT a standard switch size is _____ amps.

    A. 30 B. 40 C. 60 D. 100

29. A NEMAl Enclosure for a safety switch or circuit breaker should be used _____ areas.

    A. outdoors, in non-hazardous
    B. outdoors, in hazardous
    C. indoors, in wet
    D. indoors, in dry general-purpose

30. Of the following abbreviations, the one which a main-tainer would LEAST expect to encounter in the course of his duties is

    A. E.M.F. B. M.S.T. C. H.T. D. M.C.M.

KEY (CORRECT ANSWERS)

1.	B	16.	A
2.	C	17.	C
3.	A	18.	A
4.	B	19.	A
5.	B	20.	A
6.	B	21.	A
7.	C	22.	D
8.	D	23.	B
9.	D	24.	A
10.	C	25.	B
11.	A	26.	C
12.	C	27.	A
13.	D	28.	B
14.	B	29.	D
15.	B	30.	B

TEST 2

DIRECTIONS: Each question or incomplete statement is followed by several suggested answers or completions. Select the one that BEST answers the question or completes the statement. *PRINT THE LETTER OF THE CORRECT ANSWER IN THE SPACE AT THE RIGHT.*

Questions 1-3.

DIRECTIONS: Questions 1 through 3 are based on the table of instruments listed below:
  I. ammeter
  II. megger
  III. voltmeter
  IV. wattmeter
  V. ohmmeter
  VI. power factor meter

1. The instrument that should be used to measure the insulation resistance of a cable is number

    A. I   B. II   C. III   D. IV

2. The instrument that should be used to measure the resistance of a IK resistor is number

    A. I   B. IV   C. V   D. VI

3. The instrument that should be used to measure the power dissipated in a circuit is number

    A. II   B. III   C. IV   D. VI

4. In opening or closing an 11,000-volt disconnect switch, a maintainer should use an approved

    A. plastic pipe   B. insulated switch stick
    C. link   D. ground wire

5. To allow for control of a lighting fixture from two locations, a maintainer should install two _____ switches.

    A. single-pole   B. double-pole
    C. three-way   D. four-way

6. The power dissipated by a 12-ohm heater in a 120-volt circuit is _____ watts.

    A. 600   B. 740   C. 1200   D. 1440

7. For a given A.C. circuit, the ratio of KW to KVA is known as the

    A. efficiency   B. transformer ratio
    C. useful power   D. power fa tor

8. The color used for the series wire in incandescent series lighting installations is

    A. black   B. green   C. red   D. white

9. When pulling three single-conductor, rubber-covered wires through a conduit, it is GOOD practice to pull

   A. through one wire at a time
   B. only one wire through first to clear the conduit and then pull the other two wires through
   C. two wires through first to prevent damage to the rubber and then pull the third wire through
   D. all three wires through at the same time

Questions 10-13.

DIRECTIONS: Questions 10 through 13 are based on the wiring diagram below. In answering these questions, use ONLY the information given below.

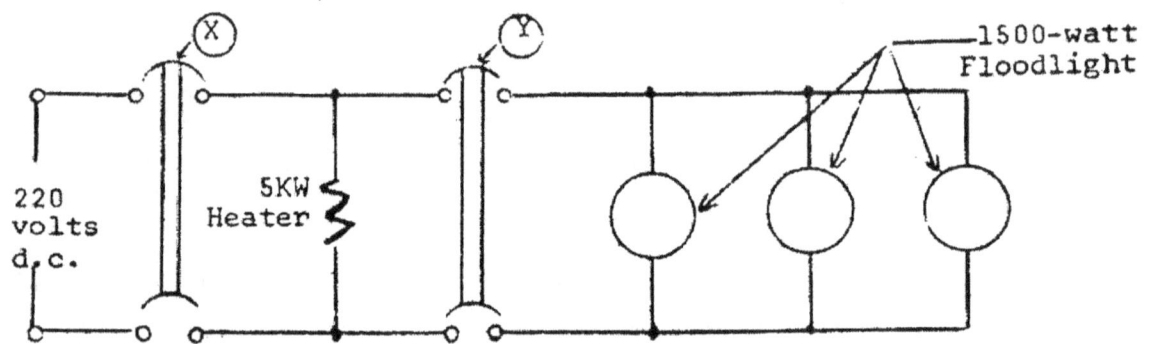

10. The current drawn by each floodlight is APPROXIMATELY _____ amps.

    A. 2.3   B. 6.8   C. 22.7   D. 24.6

11. The size of circuit breaker J should be _____ amps.

    A. 15   B. 20   C. 30   D. 50

12. The current drawn by the 5KW heater should be APPROXIMATELY _____ amps.

    A. 45.5   B. 22.7   C. 18.6   D. 5.0

13. The size of circuit breaker X should be _____ amps.

    A. 15   B. 20   C. 40   D. D, 50

14. When using a Hickey to bend conduit, it is GOOD practice to

    A. stand off to the side of the Hickey handle in case it slips
    B. make a ninety-degree bend in one stroke to save time and effort
    C. stand directly in back of the Hickey handle for maximum leverage
    D. apply the Hickey at the exact length required so as not to waste conduit

15. If a maintainer is receiving verbal orders from his foreman which conflict with standard safety practices, the maintainer should

    A. ask for advice from another foreman
    B. immediately call it to the attention of his foreman

C. follow the practice which makes the most sense to him
D. bring this to the attention of his assistant supervisor

16. Electric service switch enclosures are usually grounded to the water line to

    A. prevent electrolysis
    B. insure full line voltage
    C. simplify wiring
    D. reduce the shock hazard

17. The secondary of a single-phase lighting transformer should ALWAYS have

    A. both legs fused
    B. both legs unfused
    C. one leg grounded
    D. both legs grounded

18. A type of conduit fitting that should be used for a right-angle bend is a(n) _____ condu-let.

    A. LL
    B. C
    C. A
    D. E

19. Cartridge fuses, up to a rating of 60 amperes, NORMALLY have _____ contacts.

    A. knife blade
    B. ferrule
    C. screw-type
    D. plug-type

20. The type of socket NORMALLY used with incandescent lamps rated from 300 watts to 1500 watts has a(n) _____ base.

    A. candelabra
    B. medium
    C. mogul
    D. Edison

21. One reason why D.C. operation is preferred to A.C. operation of fluorescent lamps is that

    A. D.C. operation eliminates any power factor problem
    B. D.C. operation requires less special auxiliary equipment
    C. A.C. operation results in a shorter life span of the lamps
    D. A.C. operation gives less overall efficiency of light production

22. A flagman observes a train approaching. He receives the *all clear* signal but notices an unsafe condition on the track.
    The flagman MUST

    A. wave a yellow flag
    B. use hand signals
    C. blow his whistle
    D. leave the stop in the tripped position

23. Of the following, the flagging signal color that is CORRECTLY defined is:

    A. Red - proceed slowly and be prepared to stop
    B. White - proceed at a speed of 30 miles per hour
    C. Green - proceed at a speed not to exceed 5 miles per hour
    D. Yellow - proceed at a speed not to exceed 10 miles per hour

24. The BEST tool for bending two-inch conduit is a

    A. hydraulic bender
    B. Hickey
    C. pipe wrench
    D. mandrel

25. Of the following tools or pieces of equipment, the one that a flagman is required to use is a 25.____

   A. link chain
   B. piece of stout cord
   C. hammer
   D. C clamp

KEY (CORRECT ANSWERS)

1. B
2. C
3. C
4. B
5. C

6. C
7. D
8. C
9. D
10. B

11. C
12. B
13. D
14. A
15. B

16. D
17. C
18. A
19. B
20. C

21. A
22. D
23. D
24. A
25. B

TEST 3

DIRECTIONS: Each question or incomplete statement is followed by several suggested answers or completions. Select the one that BEST answers the question or completes the statement. *PRINT THE LETTER OF THE CORRECT ANSWER IN THE SPACE AT THE RIGHT.*

Questions 1-4.

DIRECTIONS: Questions 1 through 4 are based on the drawing below. The drawing is part of a lighting plan.

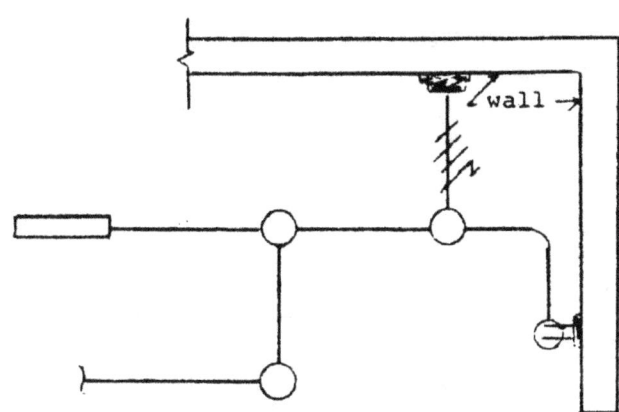

1. The symbol  represents a

   A. fluorescent lamp
   B. power panel board
   C. safety switch
   D. lighting panel board

   1.____

2. The symbol  represents

   A. a three-phase circuit
   B. 4 live wires in a conduit
   C. three phases and a neutral wire
   D. 3 live wires and a neutral in a conduit

   2.____

3. The symbol ⬜ represents a(n)

   A. motor
   B. incandescent lighting fixture
   C. fluorescent lighting fixture
   D. telephone cabinet

   3.____

4. The symbol represents a(n)

   A. receptacle
   B. incandescent lighting fixture
   C. exit light fixture
   D. emergency telephone

   4.____

63

5. If it appears to a flagman that a train is going to pass the flagman's stop signal, the flagman should

   A. remove the portable train stop
   B. sound a succession of short blasts of his signal whistle
   C. remove the white and yellow flags
   D. conceal his red flag from the motorman's view

Questions 6-11.

DIRECTIONS: Based on the diagram shown below, answer Questions 6 through 11. Unless otherwise stated, assume that all' switches are open. Each resistor has a resistance of 20 ohms. Ignore the effect of the resistance of the ammeter and the voltmeter on the circuit.

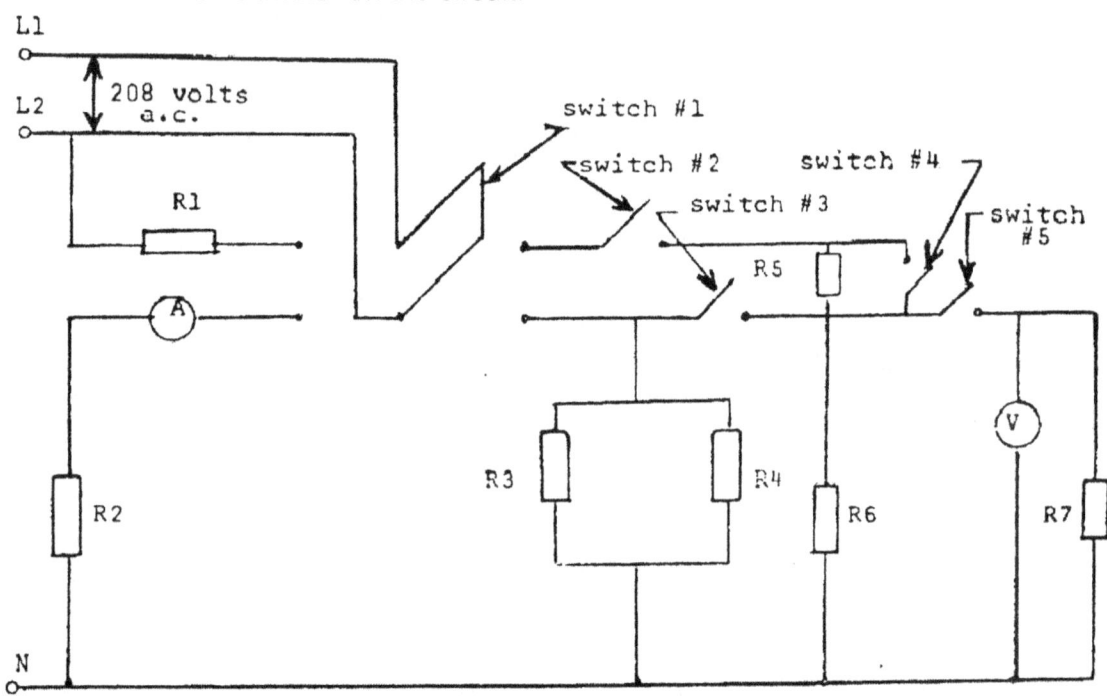

6. Switch #1 is a _____ switch.

   A. single-pole, single-throw
   B. double-pole, single-throw
   C. double-pole, double-throw
   D. three-way

7. If switch #1 is closed to the left, the current indicated by the ammeter should be APPROXIMATELY _____ amps,

   A. 5.2   B. 6.0   C. 10.4   D. 20.8

8. If switch #1 is closed to the left, the power dissipated by resistor Rl should be APPROXIMATELY _____ watts.

   A. 240   B. 720   C. 1,080   D. 2,160

9. If switch #1 is closed to the right and switch #3 is closed, the equivalent circuit resistance is MOST NEARLY _____ ohms.

   A. 6.7   B. 10.0   C. 13.4   D. 60.0

10. If switch #1 is closed to the right and switches #2 and #5 are closed, the voltage indicated by the voltmeter should be APPROXIMATELY _____ volts.

    A. 40   B. 60   C. 70   D. 120

11. If switch #1 is closed to the right, the following group of switches that should NOT be closed is switches

    A. #2, 3, and 5
    B. #2, 4, and 5
    C. #2, 3, and 4
    D. #3, 4, and 5

12. When a maintainer is cutting conduit with a hacksaw, the cutting speed should be APPROXIMATELY _____ strokes per minute.

    A. 10   B. 20   C. 60   D. 120

13. The size of the nail used in fastening two 2" x 4" wood studs together should be

    A. 2d   B. 3d   C. 5d   D. 10d

14. Lag screws should be tighted with a(n)

    A. pair of pliers
    B. pipe wrench
    C. open-end wrench
    D. box wrench

15. When a maintainer is cutting external threads on a piece of conduit, he should use a

    A. tap
    B. die
    C. drill
    D. tubing cutter

16. Before a hole is drilled in a steel plate, the punch that should be used is a _____ punch.

    A. starting   B. drift   C. center   D. aligning

17. The tool used to remove a burr that is inside a conduit is a

    A. drill
    B. tap
    C. reamer
    D. long-nose cutting plier

18. When opening or closing a 2,500-volt oil switch, a maintainer should wear _____ gloves over _____ gloves.

    A. leather; cotton
    B. leather; rubber
    C. cotton; rubber
    D. rubber; cotton

19. Protective safety glasses should be worn when

    A. climbing a lighting pole
    B. grinding a screwdriver tip
    C. stripping insulation from a wire
    D. installing a lighting circuit breaker in a panel

20. A maintainer has been instructed to install a convenience outlet on an existing circuit in an office.
    Of the following, he should FIRST

    A. connect the live wire to the convenience outlet
    B. connect the ground and neutral wires to the convenience outlet
    C. open, block, and tag the panel board switch feeding the circuit
    D. summon a helper or maintainer to stand by in case of an emergency

21. One APPROPRIATE way to determine whether one conductor of a three-wire, 208-volt circuit is alive is to

    A. ground the circuit with a bare wire
    B. touch this conductor quickly with your finger
    C. apply a neon tester between the other two conductors
    D. apply a neon tester between this conductor and ground

22. A group of wire sizes correctly arranged in order of *decreasing* current-carrying capacity is

    A. 4/0; 12; 16   B. 12; 2/0; 18
    C. 16; 14; 2/0   D. 14; 18; 4/0

23. A solid wire and a stranded wire will be designated by the same size if they have the same

    A. weight   B. length
    C. insulation covering D. cross-sectional area

24. When a maintainer is assigned to do a job with which he is not familiar, he should

    A. learn by doing the work
    B. ask a maintainer's helper for assistance
    C. ask his foreman to explain the work required
    D. ask another maintainer to do the work with him

25. If the total rating of installed shop equipment is 2,000 watts and the maximum demand is 1,100 watts, the demand factor is

    A. 22%   B. 31%   C. 55%   D. 182%

KEY (CORRECT ANSWERS)

1.	D	11.	C
2.	D	12.	C
3.	C	13.	D
4.	A	14.	C
5.	B	15.	B
6.	C	16.	C
7.	B	17.	C
8.	D	18.	B
9.	A	19.	B
10.	A	20.	C

21. D
22. A
23. D
24. C
25. C

EXAMINATION SECTION
TEST 1

DIRECTIONS: Each question or incomplete statement is followed by several suggested answers or completions. Select the one that BEST answers the question or completes the statement. *PRINT THE LETTER OF THE CORRECT ANSWER IN THE SPACE AT THE RIGHT.*

Questions 1-6.

DIRECTIONS: Questions 1 through 6 are to be answered on the basis of the circuit diagram below. All switches are initially open.

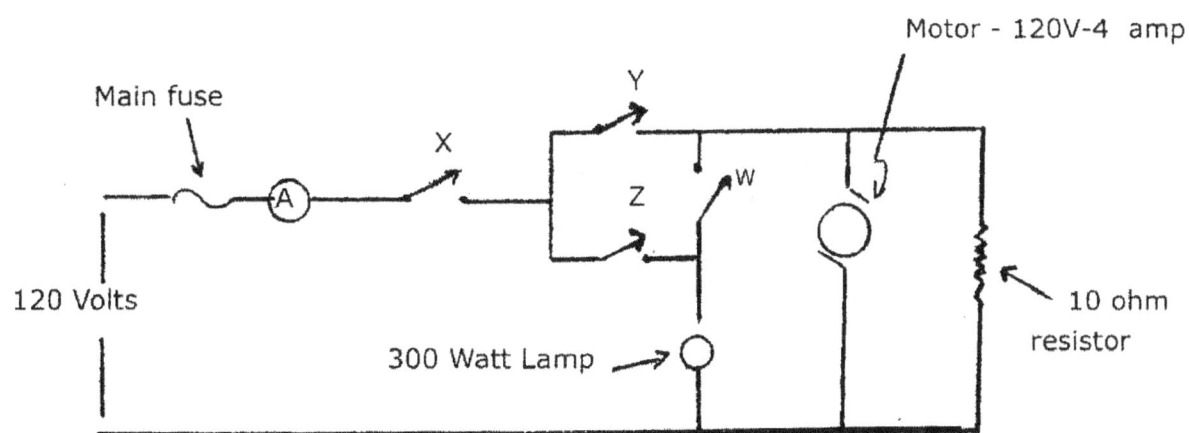

1. To light the 300 watt lamp, the following switches MUST be closed: 1.____
   A. X and Y   B. Y and Z   C. X and Z   D. X and W

2. If all of the switches W, X, Y, and Z are closed, the following will happen: 2.____
   A. The lamp will light and the motor will rotate
   B. The lamp will light and the motor will not rotate
   C. The lamp will not light and the motor will not rotate
   D. A short circuit will occur and the main fuse will blow

3. With 120 volts applied across the 10 ohm resistor, the current drawn by the resistor is _____ amp(s). 3.____
   A. 1/12   B. 1.2   C. 12   D. 1200

4. With 120 volts applied to the 10 ohm resistor, the power used by the resistor is _____ kw. 4.____
   A. 1.44   B. 1.2   C. .144   D. .12

5. The current drawn by the 300 watt lamp when lighted should be APPROXIMATELY _____ amps. 5.____
   A. 2.5   B. 3.6   C. 25   D. 36

69

6. In the circuit shown, the symbol A is used to indicate a (n)
   A. ammeter
   B. *and* circuit
   C. voltmeter
   D. wattmeter

7. Of the following materials, the BEST conductor of electricity is
   A. iron
   B. copper
   C. aluminum
   D. glass

8. The sum of 6'6", 5'9", and 2' 1 1/2" is
   A. 13'4 1/2"
   B. 13'6 1/2"
   C. 14'4 1/2"
   D. 14'6 1/2"

9.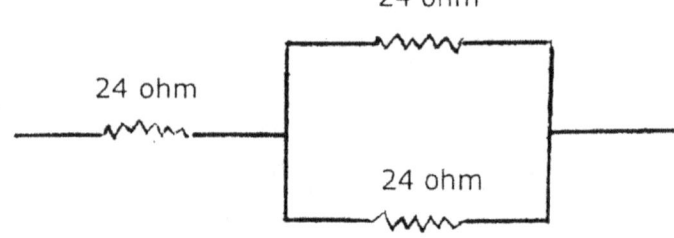

   The equivalent resistance of the three resistors shown in the sketch above is _____ ohms.
   A. 8
   B. 24
   C. 36
   D. 72

10.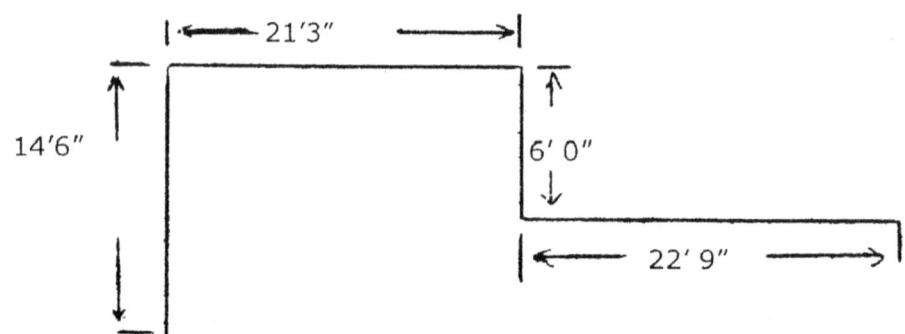

    The TOTAL length of electrical conduit that must be run along the path shown on the diagram above is
    A. 63'8"
    B. 64'6"
    C. 65'6"
    D. 66'8"

11. Of the following electrical devices, the one that is NOT normally used in direct current electrical circuits is a (n)
    A. circuit breaker
    B. double-pole switch
    C. transformer
    D. inverter

12. The number of 120-volt light bulbs that should NORMALLY be connected in series across a 600-volt electric line is
    A. 1
    B. 2
    C. 3
    D. 5

13. Of the following motors, the one that does NOT have any brushes is the _____ motor.

    A. d.c. shunt
    B. d.c. series
    C. squirrel cage induction
    D. compound

14. Of the following materials, the one that is COMMONLY used as an electric heating element in an electric heater is

    A. zinc
    B. brass
    C. terne plate
    D. nichrome

Questions 15-25.

DIRECTIONS: Questions 15 through 25 are to be answered on the basis of the instruments listed below. Each instrument is listed with an identifying number in front of it.

    1 - Hygrometer
    2 - Ammeter
    3 - Voltmeter
    4 - Wattmeter
    5 - Megger
    6 - Oscilloscope
    7 - Frequency meter
    8 - Micrometer
    9 - Vernier caliper
    10 - Wire gage
    11 - 6-foot folding rule
    12 - Architect's scale
    13 - Planimeter
    14 - Engineer's scale
    15 - Ohmmeter

15. The instrument that should be used to accurately measure the resistance of a 4,700 ohm resistor is Number

    A. 3   B. 4   C. 7   D. 15

16. To measure the current in an electrical circuit, the instrument that should be used is Number

    A. 2   B. 7   C. 8   D. 15

17. To measure the insulation resistance of a rubber-covered electrical cable, the instrument that should be used is Number

    A. 4   B. 5   C. 8   D. 15

18. An AC motor is hooked up to a power distribution box.
    In order to check the voltage at the motor terminals, the instrument that should be used is Number

    A. 2   B. 3   C. 4   D. 7

19. To measure the shaft diameter of a motor accurately to one-thousandth of an inch, the instrument that should be used is Number

    A. 8   B. 10   C. 11   D. 14

20. The instrument that should be used to determine whether 25 Hz. or 60 Hz. is present in an electrical circuit is Number

    A. 4   B. 5   C. 7   D. 8

21. Of the following, the PROPER instrument to use to determine the diameter of the conductor of a piece of electrical hook-up wire is Number

    A. 10   B. 11   C. 12   D. 14

22. The amount of electrical power being used in a balanced three-phase circuit should be measured with Number

    A. 2   B. 3   C. 4   D. 5

23. The electrical wave form at a given point in an electronic circuit can be observed with Number

    A. 2   B. 3   C. 6   D. 7

24. The PROPER instrument to use for measuring the width of a door is Number

    A. 11   B. 12   C. 13   D. 14

25. A one-inch hole with a tolerance of plus or minus three-thousandths is reamed in a steel block.
    The PROPER instrument to use to accurately check the diameter of the hole is Number

    A. 8   B. 9   C. 11   D. 14

KEY (CORRECT ANSWERS)

1. C	11. C
2. A	12. D
3. C	13. C
4. A	14. D
5. A	15. D
6. A	16. A
7. B	17. B
8. C	18. B
9. C	19. A
10. B	20. C

21. A
22. C
23. C
24. A
25. B

TEST 2

DIRECTIONS: Each question or incomplete statement is followed by several suggested answers or completions. Select the one that BEST answers the question or completes the statement. *PRINT THE LETTER OF THE CORRECT ANSWER IN THE SPACE AT THE RIGHT.*

1. The number of conductors required to connect a 3-phase delta connected heater bank to an electric power panel board is

   A. 2   B. 3   C. 4   D. 5

2. Of the following, the wire size that is MOST commonly used for branch lighting circuits in homes is _____ A.W.G.

   A. #12   B. #8   C. #6   D. #4

3. When installing electrical circuits, the tool that should be used to pull wire through a conduit is a

   A. mandrel
   B. snake
   C. rod
   D. pulling iron

4. Of the following AC voltages, the LOWEST voltage that a neon test lamp can detect is _____ volts.

   A. 6   B. 12   C. 80   D. 120

5. Of the following, the BEST procedure to use when storing tools that are subject to rusting is to

   A. apply a thin coating of soap onto the tools
   B. apply a light coating of oil to the tools
   C. wrap the tools in clean cheesecloth
   D. place the tools in a covered container

6. If a 3 1/2 inch long nail is required to nail wood framing members together, the nail size to use should be

   A. 2d   B. 4d   C. 16d   D. 60d

7. Of the four motors listed below, the one that can operate only on alternating current is a(n) _____ motor.

   A. series
   B. shunt
   C. compound
   D. induction

8. The sum of 1/3 + 2/5 + 5/6 is

   A. 1 17/30   B. 1 3/5   C. 1 15/24   D. 1 5/6

9. Of the following instruments, the one that should be used to measure the state of charge of a lead-acid storage battery is a(n)

   A. ammeter
   B. ohmmeter
   C. hydrometer
   D. thermometer

10. If three 1 1/2 volt dry cell batteries are wired in series, the TOTAL voltage provided by the three batteries is _____ volts.

   A. 1.5 B. 3 C. 4.5 D. 6.0

11. Taking into account time and one-half payment for time over 40 hours of work, the gross pay of an employee who works 43 hours in a week at a rate of pay of $10.68 per hour is

   A. $427.20 B. $459.24 C. $475.26 D. $491.28

12. The sum of 0.365 + 3.941 + 10.676 + 0.784 is

   A. 13.766 B. 15.666 C. 15.756 D. 15.766

13. In order to transmit mechanical power between two rotating shafts at right angles to each other, two gears are used. Of the following, the type of gears that should be used are _____ gears.

   A. herringbone
   B. spur
   C. bevel
   D. rack and pinion

14. To properly ground the service electrical equipment in a building, a ground connection should be made to _____ the building.

   A. the waste or soil line leaving
   B. the vent line going to the exterior of
   C. any steel beam in
   D. the cold water line entering

15. The area of the triangle shown at the right is _____ square inches.
   A. 120
   B. 240
   C. 360
   D. 480

Questions 16-25.

DIRECTIONS: Questions 16 through 25 are to be answered on the basis of the tools shown on the next page. The tools are not shown to scale. Each tool is shown with an identifying number alongside it.

3 (#2)

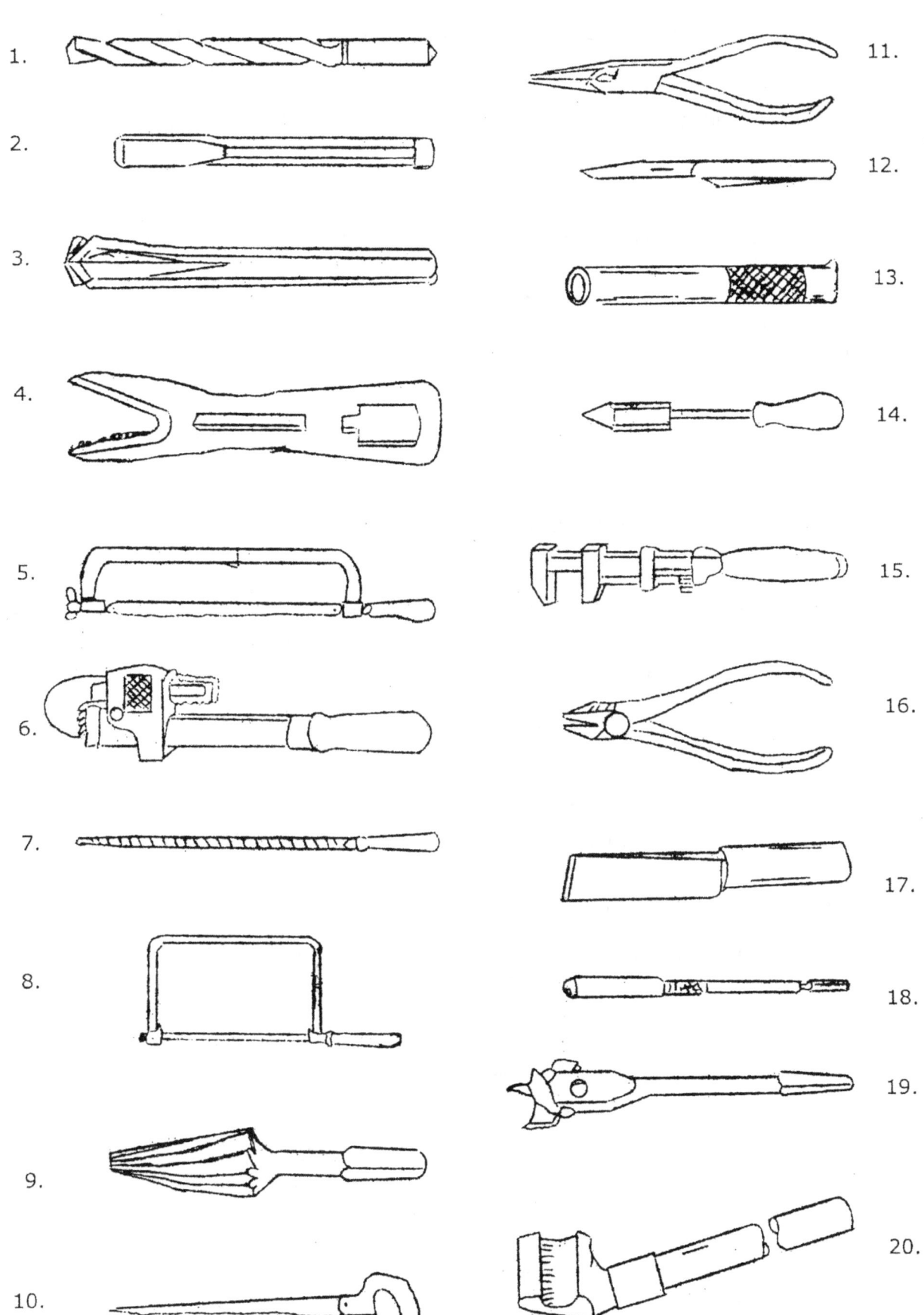

16. The tool that should be used for cutting thin wall steel conduit is Number 16._____
    A. 5   B. 8   C. 10   D. 16

17. The tool that should be used for cutting a 1 7/8 inch diameter hole in a wood joist is Number 17._____
    A. 3   B. 9   C. 14   D. 19

18. The tool that should be used for soldering splices in electrical wire is Number 18._____
    A. 3   B. 7   C. 13   D. 14

19. After cutting off a piece of 3/4 inch diameter electrical conduit, the tool that should be used for removing a burr from the inside of the conduit is Number 19._____
    A. 9   B. 11   C. 12   D. 14

20. The tool that should be used for turning a coupling onto a threaded conduit is Number 20._____
    A. 6   B. 11   C. 15   D. 16

21. The tool that should be used for cutting wood lathing in plaster walls is Number 21._____
    A. 5   B. 7   C. 10   D. 12

22. The tool that should be used for drilling a 3/8 inch diameter hole in a steel beam is Number 22._____
    A. 1   B. 2   C. 3   D. 9

23. Of the following, the BEST tool to use for stripping insulation from electrical hook-up wire is Number 23._____
    A. 11   B. 12   C. 15   D. 20

24. The tool that should be used for bending an electrical wire around a terminal post is Number 24._____
    A. 4   B. 11   C. 15   D. 16

25. The tool that should be used for cutting electrical hookup wire is Number 25._____
    A. 5   B. 12   C. 16   D. 17

KEY (CORRECT ANSWERS)

1. B
2. A
3. B
4. C
5. B

6. C
7. D
8. A
9. C
10. C

11. C
12. D
13. C
14. D
15. A

16. A
17. D
18. D
19. A
20. A

21. C
22. A
23. B
24. B
25. C

TEST 3

DIRECTIONS: Each question or incomplete statement is followed by several suggested answers or completions. Select the one that BEST answers the question or completes the statement. *PRINT THE LETTER OF THE CORRECT ANSWER IN THE SPACE AT THE RIGHT.*

1. An electric circuit has current flowing through it. The panel board switch feeding the circuit is opened, causing arcing across the switch contacts.
   Generally, this arcing is caused by

   A. a lack of energy storage in the circuit
   B. electrical energy stored by a capacitor
   C. electrical energy stored by a resistor
   D. magnetic energy induced by an inductance

   1.____

2. MOST filter capacitors in radios have a capacity rating given in

   A. microvolts   B. milliamps
   C. millihenries   D. microfarads

   2.____

3. Of the following, the electrical wire size that is COMMONLY used for telephone circuits is _____ A.W.G.

   A. #6   B. #10   C. #12   D. #22

   3.____

Questions 4-9.

DIRECTIONS: Questions 4 through 9 are to be answered on the basis of the electrical circuit diagram shown below, where letters are used to identify various circuit components.

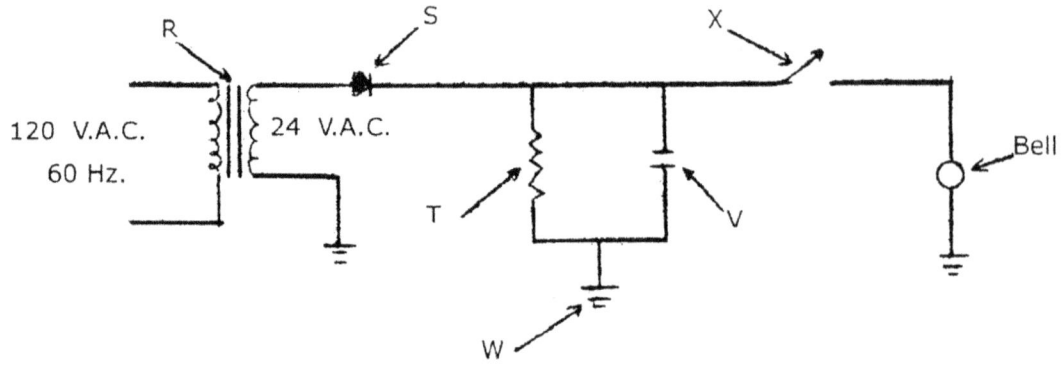

4. The device indicated by the letter R is a

   A. capacitor   B. converter
   C. resistor   D. transformer

   4.____

5. The device indicated by the letter S is a

   A. transistor   B. diode
   C. thermistor   D. directional relay

   5.____

6. The devices indicated by the letters T and V are used together to _____ components of the secondary current.

   A. reduce the AC
   B. reduce the DC
   C. transform the AC
   D. invert the AC

7. The letter W points to a standard electrical symbol for a

   A. wire
   B. ground
   C. terminal
   D. lightning arrestor

8. Closing switch X will apply the following type of voltage to the bell:

   A. 60 Hz. AC
   B. DC
   C. pulsating AC
   D. 120 Hz. AC

9. The circuit shown contains a _____ rectifier.

   A. mercury-arc
   B. full-wave
   C. bridge
   D. half-wave

10. A bolt specified as 1/4-28 means the following:
    The

    A. bolt is 1/4 inch in diameter and has 28 threads per inch
    B. bolt is 1/4 inch in diameter and is 2.8 inches long
    C. bolt is 1/4 inch long and has 28 threads
    D. threaded portion of the bolt is 1/4 inch long and has 28 threads per inch

11. When cutting 0.045-inch thickness sheet metal, it is BEST to use a hacksaw blade that has _____ teeth per inch.

    A. 7   B. 12   C. 18   D. 32

12. To accurately tighten a bolt to 28 foot-pounds, it is BEST to use a(n) _____ wrench.

    A. pipe   B. open end   C. box   D. torque

13. When bending a 2-inch diameter conduit, the CORRECT tool to use is a

    A. hickey
    B. pipe wrench
    C. hydraulic bender
    D. stock and die

14. When soldering two #20 A.W.G. copper wires together to form a splice, the solder that SHOULD be used is _____ solder.

    A. acid-core
    B. solid-core
    C. rosin-core
    D. liquid

15. A bathroom heating unit draws 10 amperes at 115 volts.
    The hot resistance of the heating unit should be _____ ohms.

    A. .08   B. 8   C. 11.5   D. 1150

16. Of the following materials, the one that is NOT suitable as an electrical insulator is

    A. glass   B. mica   C. rubber   D. platinum

17. An air conditioning unit is rated at 1000 watts. The unit is run for 10 hours per day, five days per week.
    If the cost for electrical energy is 5 cents per kilowatt-hour, the weekly cost for electricity should be

    A. 25¢ B. 50¢ C. $2.50 D. $25.00

18. If a fuse is protecting the circuit of a 15 ohm electric heater and it is designed to blow out at a current exceeding 10 amperes, the MAXIMUM voltage from among the following that should be applied across the terminals of the heater is _____ volts.

    A. 110 B. 120 C. 160 D. 600

19. Before opening a pneumatic hose connection, it is important to remove pressure from the hose line PRIMARILY to avoid

    A. losing air
    B. personal injury
    C. damage to the hose connection
    D. a build-up of pressure in the air compressor

20. If the scale on a shop drawing is 1/4 inch to the foot, then a part which measures 3 3/8 inches long on the drawing has an ACTUAL length of _____ feet _____ inches.

    A. 12; 6 B. 13; 6 C. 13; 9 D. 14; 9

21. The function that is USUALLY performed by a motor controller is to

    A. start and stop a motor
    B. protect a motor from a short circuit
    C. prevent bearing failure of a motor
    D. control the brush wear in a motor

22. Of the following galvanized sheet metal electrical outlet boxes, the one that is NOT a commonly used size is the _____ box.

    A. 4" square
    B. 4" octagonal
    C. 4" x 2 1/8"
    D. 4" x 1"

23. When soldering a transistor into a circuit, it is MOST important to protect the transistor from

    A. the application of an excess of rosin flux
    B. excessive heat
    C. the application of an excess of solder
    D. too much pressure

24. When installing BX type cable, it is important to protect the wires in the cable from the cut ends of the armored sheath.
    The APPROVED method of providing this protection is to

    A. use a fiber or plastic insulating bushing
    B. file the cut ends of the sheath smooth
    C. use a connector where the cable enters a junction box
    D. tie the wires into an Underwriter's knot

25. While lifting a heavy piece of equipment off the floor, a person should NOT 25.____

    A. twist his body
    B. grasp it firmly
    C. maintain a solid footing on the ground
    D. bend his knees

26. It is important that metal cabinets and panels that house electrical equipment should be grounded PRIMARILY in order to 26.____

    A. prevent short circuits from occurring
    B. keep all circuits at ground potential
    C. minimize shock hazards
    D. reduce the effects of electrolytic corrosion

27. A foreman explains a technical procedure to a new employee. If the employee does not understand the instructions he has received, it would be BEST if he were to 27.____

    A. follow the procedure as best he could
    B. ask the foreman to explain it to him again
    C. avoid following the procedure
    D. ask the foreman to give him other work

28. Of the following, the BEST connectors to use when mounting an electrical panel box directly onto a concrete wall are 28.____

    A. threaded studs   B. machine screws
    C. lag screws   D. expansion bolts

29. Of the following, the BEST instrument to use to measure the small gap between relay contacts is 29.____

    A. a micrometer   B. a feeler gage
    C. inside calipers   D. a plug gage

30. A POSSIBLE result of mounting a 40 ampere fuse in a fuse box for a circuit requiring a 20 ampere fuse is that the 40 ampere fuse may 30.____

    A. provide twice as much protection to the circuit from overloads
    B. blow more easily than the smaller fuse due to an overload
    C. cause serious damage to the circuit from an overload
    D. reduce power consumption in the circuit

KEY (CORRECT ANSWERS)

1.	D	16.	D
2.	D	17.	C
3.	D	18.	B
4.	D	19.	B
5.	B	20.	B
6.	A	21.	A
7.	B	22.	D
8.	B	23.	B
9.	D	24.	A
10.	A	25.	A
11.	D	26.	C
12.	D	27.	B
13.	C	28.	D
14.	C	29.	B
15.	C	30.	C

EXAMINATION SECTION
TEST 1

DIRECTIONS: The questions in this test refer to the use of tools shown below. Read the question, and for the operation given, select the proper tool to be used from those shown. *PRINT* on your answer sheet, in the correspondingly numbered item space, the letter given below your selected tool.

KEY: CORRECT ANSWERS APPEAR AT THE END OF THIS TEST.

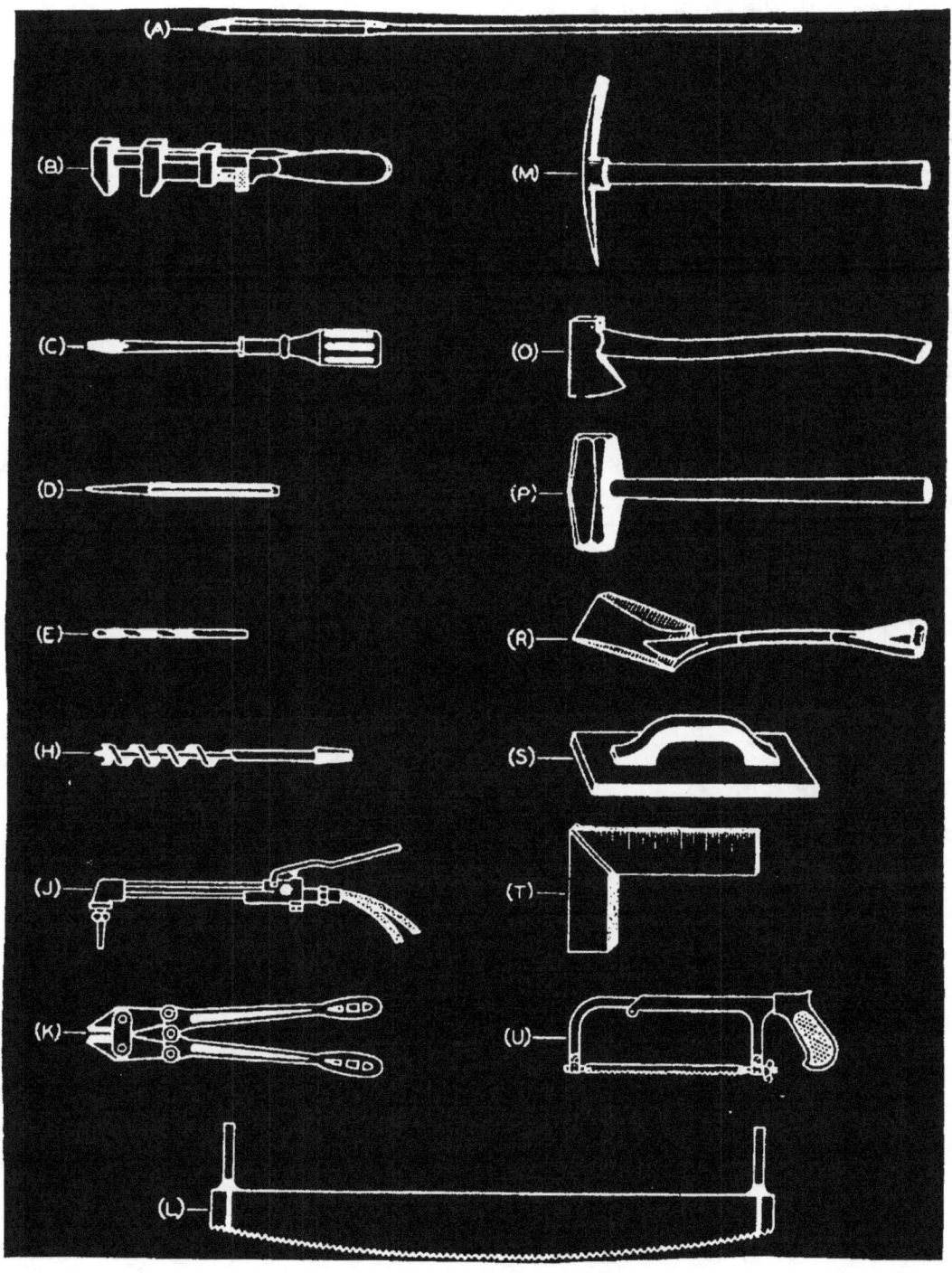

1. Sawing off the end of a bolt
2. Drilling a hole in a steel plate
3. Cutting scrap rail quickly into short lengths
4. Mixing concrete
5. Chopping off a piece of timber
6. Snipping off a piece of steel wire
7. Loading sand into a wheelbarrow
8. Loosening up a pile of solidly packed dirt and gravel
9. Drilling a large hole in a piece of timber
10. Breaking up a slab of concrete
11. Burning a hole in a piece of steel
12. Shifting a long piece of rail along the ground
13. Tightening a nut on a bolt
14. Making a straight cut through a heavy piece of timber
15. Inserting a round-head wood screw
16. Marking the center of a hole to be drilled in a steel plate
17. Determining if a piece of timber has been cut off squarely
18. Putting a smooth surface on concrete
19. Putting sharp points on the ends of wooden stakes
20. Measuring the thickness of a board

KEY (CORRECT ANSWERS)

1.	U		11.	J
2.	E		12.	A
3.	J		13.	B
4.	R		14.	L
5.	O		15.	C
6.	K		16.	D
7.	R		17.	T
8.	M		18.	S
9.	H		19.	O
10.	P		20.	T

TEST 2

TOOLS

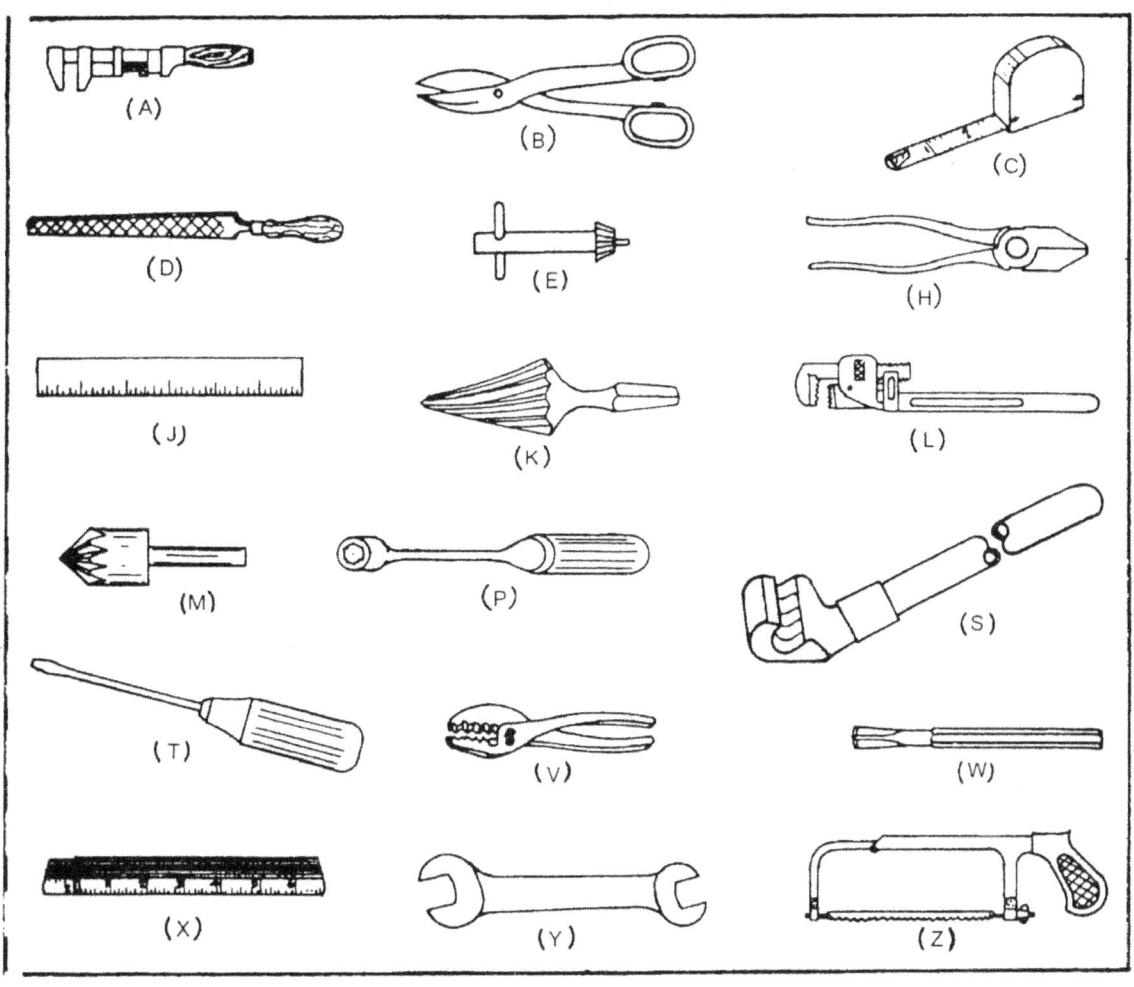

QUESTIONS

DIRECTIONS: 1 to 10 inclusive refer to the use of the tools shown above. Read the item, and, for the operation given, select the proper tool to be used from those shown. PRINT ON YOUR ANSWER SHEET, IN THE CORRESPONDINGLY NUMBERED ITEM SPACE, THE LETTER GIVEN BELOW YOUR SELECTED TOOL.

1. Loosening the nut holding a wire on a stud terminal.
2. Removing burrs from the inner edge of conduit after cutting it.
3. Measuring the distance between exposed terminals on a low-voltage switchboard.
4. Loosening a coupling which is tight on the end of a piece of conduit.
5. Tightening the chuck on an electric drill.
6. Tightening a 3/4 inch conduit bushing inside an outlet box.
7. Skinning a no. 14 A.W.G. rubber insulated wire.
8. Cutting off part of a brass machine screw which is too long.
9. Prying off a rubber gasket that is stuck to the inside of the cover that has been taken off a watertight pull box.
10. Making a hole for a lead anchor in a concrete wall.

2 (#2)

KEY (CORRECT ANSWERS)

1. P
2. K
3. X
4. L
5. E

6. V
7. H
8. Z
9. T
10. W

———

TEST 3

TOOLS

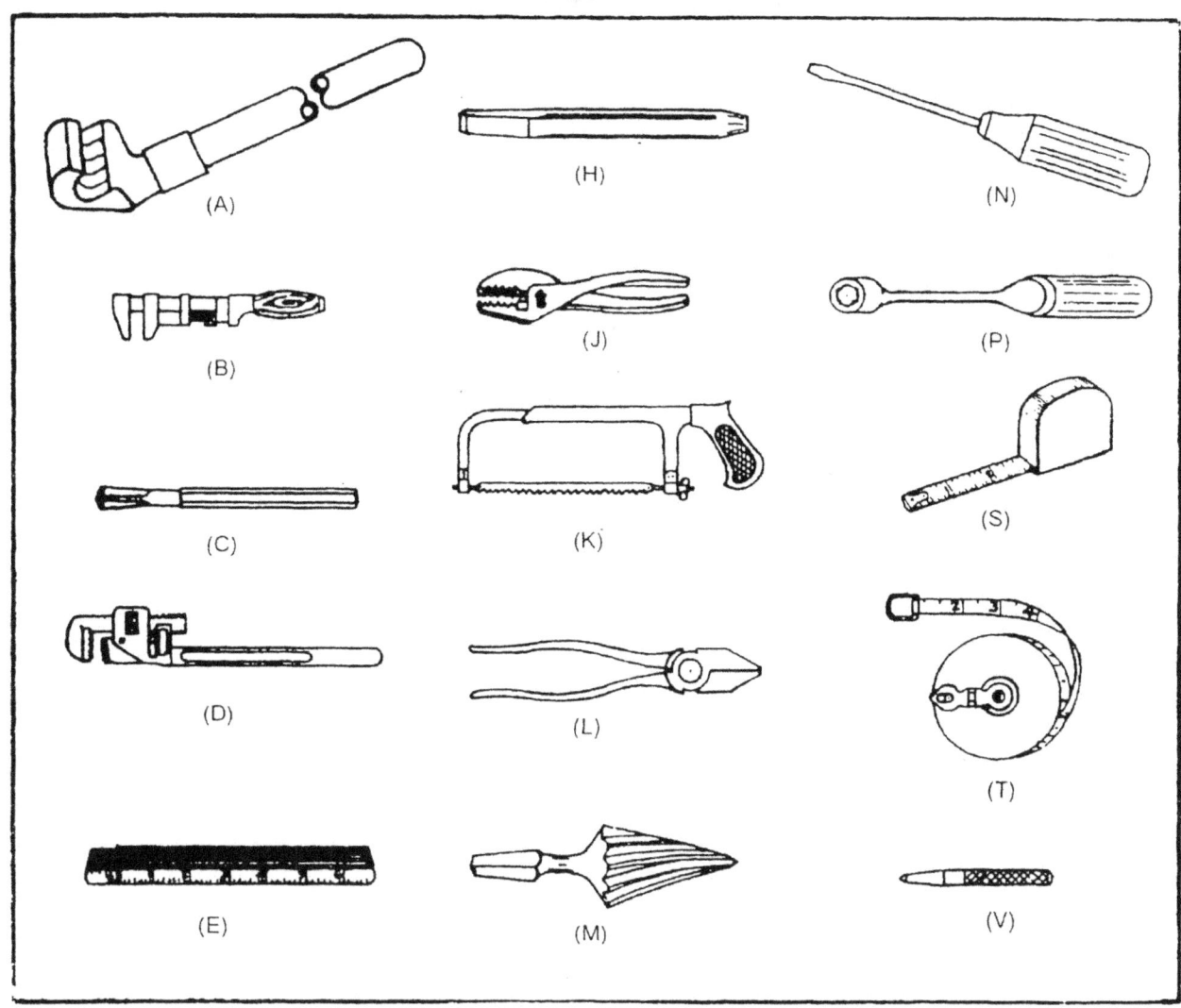

QUESTIONS

DIRECTIONS: 1 to 10 inclusive refer to the use of tools shown above. Read the item, and, for the operation given, select the proper tool to be used from those shown. *PRINT ON YOUR ANSWER SHEET, IN THE CORRESPONDINGLY NUMBERED ITEM SPACE, THE LETTER GIVEN BELOW YOUR SELECTED TOOL.*

1. Tightening a coupling on a piece of one-inch conduit.
2. Drilling a hole in a concrete wall for a lead anchor.
3. Bending a piece of 3/4-inch conduit.
4. Tightening a wire on the terminal of a standard electric light socket.
5. Cutting off a piece of 4/0 insulated copper cable.
6. Measuring the length of a proposed long conduit run.
7. Tightening a small nut on a terminal board.
8. Removing the burrs from the end of a piece of conduit after cutting.
9. Removing the flat rubber gasket stuck to the cover of a watertight pull box.
10. Knocking the head off a bolt that is rusted in place.

KEY (CORRECT ANSWERS)

1. D
2. C
3. A
4. N
5. K

6. T
7. P
8. M
9. N
10. H

ELECTRICAL TERMS AND FORMULAS

CONTENTS

	Page
TERMS	1
Agonic ...... Dielectric	1
Diode ...... Lead	2
Line of Force ...... Resistor	3
Retentivity ...... Wattmeter	4
FORMULAS	4
Ohm's Law for D-C Circuits	4
Resistors in Series	4
Resistors in Parallel	4
R-L Circuit Time Constant	5
R-C Circuit Time Constant	5
Comparison of Units in Electric and Magnetic Circuits	5
Capacitors in Series	5
Capacitors in Parallel	5
Capacitive Reactance	5
Impedance in an R-C Circuit (Series)	5
Inductors in Series	5
Inductors in Parallel	5
Inductive Reactance	5
Q of a Coil	5
Impedance of an R-L Circuit (Series)	5
Impedance with R, C, and L in Series	5
Parallel Circuit Impedance	5
Sine-Wave Voltage Relationships	5
Power in A-C Circuit	6
Transformers	6
Three-Phase Voltage and Current Relationships	6
GREEK ALPHABET	7
Alpha ...... Omega	7
COMMON ABBREVIATIONS AND LETTER SYMBOLS	8
Alternating Current (noun) ...... Watt	8

ELECTRICAL TERMS AND FORMULAS

Terms

AGONIC.—An imaginary line of the earth's surface passing through points where the magnetic declination is 0°; that is, points where the compass points to true north.

AMMETER.—An instrument for measuring the amount of electron flow in amperes.

AMPERE.—The basic unit of electrical current.

AMPERE-TURN.—The magnetizing force produced by a current of one ampere flowing through a coil of one turn.

AMPLIDYNE.—A rotary magnetic or dynamoelectric amplifier used in servomechanism and control applications.

AMPLIFICATION.—The process of increasing the strength (current, power, or voltage) of a signal.

AMPLIFIER.—A device used to increase the signal voltage, current, or power, generally composed of a vacuum tube and associated circuit called a stage. It may contain several stages in order to obtain a desired gain.

AMPLITUDE.—The maximum instantaneous value of an alternating voltage or current, measured in either the positive or negative direction.

ARC.—A flash caused by an electric current ionizing a gas or vapor.

ARMATURE.—The rotating part of an electric motor or generator. The moving part of a relay or vibrator.

ATTENUATOR.—A network of resistors used to reduce voltage, current, or power delivered to a load.

AUTOTRANSFORMER.—A transformer in which the primary and secondary are connected together in one winding.

BATTERY.—Two or more primary or secondary cells connected together electrically. The term does not apply to a single cell.

BREAKER POINTS.—Metal contacts that open and close a circuit at timed intervals.

BRIDGE CIRCUIT.—The electrical bridge circuit is a term referring to any one of a variety of electric circuit networks, one branch of which, the "bridge" proper, connects two points of equal potential and hence carries no current when the circuit is properly adjusted or balanced.

BRUSH.—The conducting material, usually a block of carbon, bearing against the commutator or sliprings through which the current flows in or out.

BUS BAR.—A primary power distribution point connected to the main power source.

CAPACITOR.—Two electrodes or sets of electrodes in the form of plates, separated from each other by an insulating material called the dielectric.

CHOKE COIL.—A coil of low ohmic resistance and high impedance to alternating current.

CIRCUIT.—The complete path of an electric current.

CIRCUIT BREAKER.—An electromagnetic or thermal device that opens a circuit when the current in the circuit exceeds a predetermined amount. Circuit breakers can be reset.

CIRCULAR MIL.—An area equal to that of a circle with a diameter of 0.001 inch. It is used for measuring the cross section of wires.

COAXIAL CABLE.—A transmission line consisting of two conductors concentric with and insulated from each other.

COMMUTATOR.—The copper segments on the armature of a motor or generator. It is cylindrical in shape and is used to pass power into or from the brushes. It is a switching device.

CONDUCTANCE.—The ability of a material to conduct or carry an electric current. It is the reciprocal of the resistance of the material, and is expressed in mhos.

CONDUCTIVITY.—The ease with which a substance transmits electricity.

CONDUCTOR.—Any material suitable for carrying electric current.

CORE.—A magnetic material that affords an easy path for magnetic flux lines in a coil.

COUNTER E.M.F.—Counter electromotive force; an e.m.f. induced in a coil or armature that opposes the applied voltage.

CURRENT LIMITER.—A protective device similar to a fuse, usually used in high amperage circuits.

CYCLE.—One complete positive and one complete negative alternation of a current or voltage.

DIELECTRIC.—An insulator; a term that refers to the insulating material between the plates of a capacitor.

ELECTRICAL TERMS AND FORMULAS

DIODE.—Vacuum tube—a two element tube that contains a cathode and plate; semiconductor—a material of either germanium or silicon that is manufactured to allow current to flow in only one direction. Diodes are used as rectifiers and detectors.

DIRECT CURRENT.—An electric current that flows in one direction only.

EDDY CURRENT.—Induced circulating currents in a conducting material that are caused by a varying magnetic field.

EFFICIENCY.—The ratio of output power to input power, generally expressed as a percentage.

ELECTROLYTE.—A solution of a substance which is capable of conducting electricity. An electrolyte may be in the form of either a liquid or a paste.

ELECTROMAGNET.—A magnet made by passing current through a coil of wire wound on a soft iron core.

ELECTROMOTIVE FORCE (e.m.f.).—The force that produces an electric current in a circuit.

ELECTRON.—A negatively charged particle of matter.

ENERGY.—The ability or capacity to do work.

FARAD.—The unit of capacitance.

FEEDBACK.—A transfer of energy from the output circuit of a device back to its input.

FIELD.—The space containing electric or magnetic lines of force.

FIELD WINDING.—The coil used to provide the magnetizing force in motors and generators.

FLUX FIELD.—All electric or magnetic lines of force in a given region.

FREE ELECTRONS.—Electrons which are loosely held and consequently tend to move at random among the atoms of the material.

FREQUENCY.—The number of complete cycles per second existing in any form of wave motion; such as the number of cycles per second of an alternating current.

FULL-WAVE RECTIFIER CIRCUIT.—A circuit which utilizes both the positive and the negative alternations of an alternating current to produce a direct current.

FUSE.—A protective device inserted in series with a circuit. It contains a metal that will melt or break when current is increased beyond a specific value for a definite period of time.

GAIN.—The ratio of the output power, voltage, or current to the input power, voltage, or current, respectively.

GALVANOMETER.—An instrument used to measure small d-c currents.

GENERATOR.—A machine that converts mechanical energy into electrical energy.

GROUND.—A metallic connection with the earth to establish ground potential. Also, a common return to a point of zero potential. The chassis of a receiver or a transmitter is sometimes the common return, and therefore the ground of the unit.

HENRY.—The basic unit of inductance.

HORSEPOWER.—The English unit of power, equal to work done at the rate of 550 foot-pounds per second. Equal to 746 watts of electrical power.

HYSTERESIS.—A lagging of the magnetic flux in a magnetic material behind the magnetizing force which is producing it.

IMPEDANCE.—The total opposition offered to the flow of an alternating current. It may consist of any combination of resistance, inductive reactance, and capacitive reactance.

INDUCTANCE.—The property of a circuit which tends to oppose a change in the existing current.

INDUCTION.—The act or process of producing voltage by the relative motion of a magnetic field across a conductor.

INDUCTIVE REACTANCE.—The opposition to the flow of alternating or pulsating current caused by the inductance of a circuit. It is measured in ohms.

INPHASE.—Applied to the condition that exists when two waves of the same frequency pass through their maximum and minimum values of like polarity at the same instant.

INVERSELY.—Inverted or reversed in position or relationship.

ISOGONIC LINE.—An imaginary line drawn through points on the earth's surface where the magnetic deviation is equal.

JOULE.—A unit of energy or work. A joule of energy is liberated by one ampere flowing for one second through a resistance of one ohm.

KILO.—A prefix meaning 1,000.

LAG.—The amount one wave is behind another in time; expressed in electrical degrees.

LAMINATED CORE.—A core built up from thin sheets of metal and used in transformers and relays.

LEAD.—The opposite of LAG. Also, a wire or connection.

ELECTRICAL TERMS AND FORMULAS

LINE OF FORCE.—A line in an electric or magnetic field that shows the direction of the force.

LOAD.—The power that is being delivered by any power producing device. The equipment that uses the power from the power producing device.

MAGNETIC AMPLIFIER.—A saturable reactor type device that is used in a circuit to amplify or control.

MAGNETIC CIRCUIT.—The complete path of magnetic lines of force.

MAGNETIC FIELD.—The space in which a magnetic force exists.

MAGNETIC FLUX.—The total number of lines of force issuing from a pole of a magnet.

MAGNETIZE.—To convert a material into a magnet by causing the molecules to rearrange.

MAGNETO.—A generator which produces alternating current and has a permanent magnet as its field.

MEGGER.—A test instrument used to measure insulation resistance and other high resistances. It is a portable hand operated d-c generator used as an ohmmeter.

MEGOHM.—A million ohms.

MICRO.—A prefix meaning one-millionth.

MILLI.—A prefix meaning one-thousandth.

MILLIAMMETER.—An ammeter that measures current in thousandths of an ampere.

MOTOR-GENERATOR.—A motor and a generator with a common shaft used to convert line voltages to other voltages or frequencies.

MUTUAL INDUCTANCE.—A circuit property existing when the relative position of two inductors causes the magnetic lines of force from one to link with the turns of the other.

NEGATIVE CHARGE.—The electrical charge carried by a body which has an excess of electrons.

NEUTRON.—A particle having the weight of a proton but carrying no electric charge. It is located in the nucleus of an atom.

NUCLEUS.—The central part of an atom that is mainly comprised of protons and neutrons. It is the part of the atom that has the most mass.

NULL.—Zero.

OHM.—The unit of electrical resistance.

OHMMETER.—An instrument for directly measuring resistance in ohms.

OVERLOAD.—A load greater than the rated load of an electrical device.

PERMALLOY.—An alloy of nickel and iron having an abnormally high magnetic permeability.

PERMEABILITY.—A measure of the ease with which magnetic lines of force can flow through a material as compared to air.

PHASE DIFFERENCE.—The time in electrical degrees by which one wave leads or lags another.

POLARITY.—The character of having magnetic poles, or electric charges.

POLE.—The section of a magnet where the flux lines are concentrated; also where they enter and leave the magnet. An electrode of a battery.

POLYPHASE.—A circuit that utilizes more than one phase of alternating current.

POSITIVE CHARGE.—The electrical charge carried by a body which has become deficient in electrons.

POTENTIAL.—The amount of charge held by a body as compared to another point or body. Usually measured in volts.

POTENTIOMETER.—A variable voltage divider; a resistor which has a variable contact arm so that any portion of the potential applied between its ends may be selected.

POWER.—The rate of doing work or the rate of expending energy. The unit of electrical power is the watt.

POWER FACTOR.—The ratio of the actual power of an alternating or pulsating current, as measured by a wattmeter, to the apparent power, as indicated by ammeter and voltmeter readings. The power factor of an inductor, capacitor, or insulator is an expression of their losses.

PRIME MOVER.—The source of mechanical power used to drive the rotor of a generator.

PROTON.—A positively charged particle in the nucleus of an atom.

RATIO.—The value obtained by dividing one number by another, indicating their relative proportions.

REACTANCE.—The opposition offered to the flow of an alternating current by the inductance, capacitance, or both, in any circuit.

RECTIFIERS.—Devices used to change alternating current to unidirectional current. These may be vacuum tubes, semiconductors such as germanium and silicon, and dry-disk rectifiers such as selenium and copperoxide.

RELAY.—An electromechanical switching device that can be used as a remote control.

RELUCTANCE.—A measure of the opposition that a material offers to magnetic lines of force.

RESISTANCE.—The opposition to the flow of current caused by the nature and physical dimensions of a conductor.

RESISTOR.—A circuit element whose chief characteristic is resistance; used to oppose the flow of current.

ELECTRICAL TERMS AND FORMULAS

RETENTIVITY. — The measure of the ability of a material to hold its magnetism.

RHEOSTAT. — A variable resistor.

SATURABLE REACTOR. — A control device that uses a small d-c current to control a large a-c current by controlling core flux density.

SATURATION. — The condition existing in any circuit when an increase in the driving signal produces no further change in the resultant effect.

SELF-INDUCTION. — The process by which a circuit induces an e.m.f. into itself by its own magnetic field.

SERIES-WOUND. — A motor or generator in which the armature is wired in series with the field winding.

SERVO. — A device used to convert a small movement into one of greater movement or force.

SERVOMECHANISM. — A closed-loop system that produces a force to position an object in accordance with the information that originates at the input.

SOLENOID. — An electromagnetic coil that contains a movable plunger.

SPACE CHARGE. — The cloud of electrons existing in the space between the cathode and plate in a vacuum tube, formed by the electrons emitted from the cathode in excess of those immediately attracted to the plate.

SPECIFIC GRAVITY — The ratio between the density of a substance and that of pure water, at a given temperature.

SYNCHROSCOPE — An instrument used to indicate a difference in frequency between two a-c sources.

SYNCHRO SYSTEM. — An electrical system that gives remote indications or control by means of self-synchronizing motors.

TACHOMETER. — An instrument for indicating revolutions per minute.

TERTIARY WINDING. — A third winding on a transformer or magnetic amplifier that is used as a second control winding.

THERMISTOR. — A resistor that is used to compensate for temperature variations in a circuit.

THERMOCOUPLE. — A junction of two dissimilar metals that produces a voltage when heated.

TORQUE. — The turning effort or twist which a shaft sustains when transmitting power.

TRANSFORMER. — A device composed of two or more coils, linked by magnetic lines of force, used to transfer energy from one circuit to another.

TRANSMISSION LINES. — Any conductor or system of conductors used to carry electrical energy from its source to a load.

VARS. — Abbreviation for volt-ampere, reactive.

VECTOR. — A line used to represent both direction and magnitude.

VOLT. — The unit of electrical potential.

VOLTMETER. — An instrument designed to measure a difference in electrical potential, in volts.

WATT. — The unit of electrical power.

WATTMETER. — An instrument for measuring electrical power in watts.

Formulas

Ohm's Law for d-c Circuits

$$I = \frac{E}{R} = \frac{P}{E} = \sqrt{\frac{P}{R}}$$

$$R = \frac{E}{I} = \frac{P}{I^2} = \frac{E^2}{P}$$

$$E = IR = \frac{P}{I} = \sqrt{PR}$$

$$P = EI = \frac{E^2}{R} = I^2 R$$

Resistors in Series

$$R_T = R_1 + R_2 \ldots$$

Resistors in Parallel
Two resistors

$$R_T = \frac{R_1 R_2}{R_1 + R_2}$$

More than two

$$\frac{1}{R_T} = \frac{1}{R_1} + \frac{1}{R_2} + \frac{1}{R_3}$$

ELECTRICAL TERMS AND FORMULAS

R-L Circuit Time Constant equals
$$\frac{L \text{ (in henrys)}}{R \text{ (in ohms)}} = t \text{ (in seconds), or}$$
$$\frac{L \text{ (in microhenrys)}}{R \text{ (in ohms)}} = t \text{ (in microseconds)}$$

R-C Circuit Time Constant equals
R (ohms) X C (farads) = t (seconds)
R (megohms) x C (microfarads) = t (seconds)
R (ohms) x C (microfarads) = t (microseconds)
R (megohms) x C (micromicrofrads) = t (microseconds)

Comparison of Units in Electric and Magnetic Circuits.

	Electric circuit	Magnetic circuit
Force	Volt, E or e.m.f.	Gilberts, F, or m.m.f.
Flow	Ampere, I	Flux, Φ, in maxwells
Opposition	Ohms, R	Reluctance, R
Law	Ohm's law, $I = \frac{E}{R}$	Rowland's law $\Phi = \frac{F}{R}$
Intensity of force	Volts per cm. of length	$H = \frac{1.257 IN}{L}$, gilberts per centimeter of length
Density	Current density— for example, amperes per cm^2.	Flux density—for example, lines per cm^2., or gausses

Capacitors in Series
Two capacitors
$$C_T = \frac{C_1 C_2}{C_1 + C_2}$$

More than two
$$\frac{1}{C_T} = \frac{1}{C_1} + \frac{1}{C_2} + \frac{1}{C_3} \ldots$$

Capacitors in Parallel
$$C_T = C_1 + C_2 \ldots$$

Capacitive Reactance
$$X_c = \frac{1}{2\pi f C}$$

Impedance in an R-C Circuit (Series)
$$Z = \sqrt{R^2 + X_c^2}$$

Inductors in Series
$L_T = L_1 + L_2 \ldots$ (No coupling between coils)

Inductors in Parallel
Two inductors
$$L_T = \frac{L_1 L_2}{L_1 + L_2}$$ (No coupling between coils)

More than two
$$\frac{1}{L_T} = \frac{1}{L_1} + \frac{1}{L_2} + \frac{1}{L_3} \ldots$$ (No coupling between coils)

Inductive Reactance
$$X_L = 2\pi f L$$

Q of a Coil
$$Q = \frac{X_L}{R}$$

Impedance of an R-L Circuit (series)
$$Z = \sqrt{R^2 + X_L^2}$$

Impedance with R, C, and L in Series
$$Z = \sqrt{R^2 + (X_L - X_C)^2}$$

Parallel Circuit Impedance
$$Z = \frac{Z_1 Z_2}{Z_1 + Z_2}$$

Sine-Wave Voltage Relationships
Average value
$$E_{ave} = \frac{2}{\pi} \times E_{max} = 0.637 E_{max}$$

ELECTRICAL TERMS AND FORMULAS

Effective or r.m.s. value

$$E_{eff} = \frac{E_{max}}{\sqrt{2}} = \frac{E_{max}}{1.414} = 0.707 E_{max} = 1.11 E_{ave}$$

Maximum value

$$E_{max} = \sqrt{2} E_{eff} = 1.414 E_{eff} = 1.57 E_{ave}$$

Voltage in an a-c circuit

$$E = IZ = \frac{P}{I \times P.F.}$$

Current in an a-c circuit

$$I = \frac{E}{Z} = \frac{P}{E \times P.F.}$$

Power in A-C Circuit
  Apparent power = EI
  True power

$$P = EI \cos \theta = EI \times P.F.$$

Power factor

$$P.F. = \frac{P}{EI} = \cos \theta$$

$$\cos \theta = \frac{\text{true power}}{\text{apparent power}}$$

Transformers
  Voltage relationship

$$\frac{E}{E} = \frac{N}{N} \quad \text{or} \quad E = E \times \frac{N}{N}$$

  Current relationship

$$\frac{I_p}{I_s} = \frac{N_s}{N_p}$$

  Induced voltage

$$E_{eff} = 4.44 \, BAfN 10^{-8}$$

Turns ratio equals

$$\frac{N_p}{N_s} = \sqrt{\frac{Z_p}{Z_s}}$$

Secondary current

$$I_s = I_p \frac{N_p}{N_s}$$

Secondary voltage

$$E_s = E_p \frac{N_s}{N_p}$$

Three Phase Voltage and Current Relationships
With wye connected windings

$$E_{line} = 1.732 E_{coil} = \sqrt{3} E_{coil}$$

$$I_{line} = I_{coil}$$

With delta connected windings

$$E_{line} = E_{coil}$$

$$I_{line} = 1.732 I_{coil}$$

With wye or delta connected winding

$$P_{coil} = E_{coil} I_{coil}$$

$$P_t = 3 P_{coil}$$

$$P_t = 1.732 E_{line} I_{line}$$

(To convert to true power multiply by $\cos \theta$)

Synchronous Speed of Motor

$$r.p.m. = \frac{120 \times \text{frequency}}{\text{number of poles}}$$

GREEK ALPHABET

Name	Capital	Lower Case	Designates
Alpha	A	α	Angles.
Beta	B	β	Angles, flux density.
Gamma ...	Γ	γ	Conductivity.
Delta	Δ	δ	Variation of a quantity, increment.
Epsilon ...	E	ϵ	Base of natural logarithms (2.71828).
Zeta	Z	ζ	Impedance, coefficients, coordinates.
Eta	H	η	Hysteresis coefficient, efficiency, magnetizing force.
Theta	Θ	θ	Phase angle.
Iota	I	ι	
Kappa	K	κ	Dielectric constant, coupling coefficient, susceptibility.
Lambda ...	Λ	λ	Wavelength.
Mu	M	μ	Permeability, micro, amplification factor.
Nu	N	ν	Reluctivity.
Xi	Ξ	ξ	
Omicron...	O	o	
Pi	Π	π	3.1416
Rho	P	ρ	Resistivity.
Sigma	Σ	σ	
Tau	T	τ	Time constant, time-phase displacement.
Upsilon ...	Υ	υ	
Phi	Φ	φ	Angles, magnetic flux.
Chi	X	χ	
Psi	Ψ	ψ	Dielectric flux, phase difference.
Omega	Ω	ω	Ohms (capital), angular velocity ($2\pi f$).

COMMON ABBREVIATIONS AND LETTER SYMBOLS

Term	Abbreviation or Symbol
alternating current (noun)	a.c.
alternating-current (adj.)	a-c
ampere	a.
area	A
audiofrequency (noun)	AF
audiofrequency (adj.)	A-F
capacitance	C
capacitive reactance	X_C
centimeter	cm.
conductance	G
coulomb	Q
counterelectromotive force	c.e.m.f.
current (d-c or r.m.s. value)	I
current (instantaneous value)	i
cycles per second	c.p.s.
dielectric constant	K, k
difference in potential (d-c or r.m.s. value)	E
difference in potential (instantaneous value)	e
direct current (noun)	d.c.
direct-current (adj.)	d-c
electromotive force	e.m.f.
frequency	f
henry	h.
horsepower	hp.
impedance	Z
inductance	L
inductive reactance	X_L
kilovolt	kv.
kilovolt-ampere	kv.-a.
kilowatt	kw.
kilowatt-hour	kw.-hr.
magnetic field intensity	H
magnetomotive force	m.m.f.
megohm	M
microampere	μa.
microfarad	μf.
microhenry	μh.
micromicrofarad	$\mu\mu$f.
microvolt	μv.
milliampere	ma.
millihenry	mh.
milliwatt	mw.
mutual inductance	M
power	P
resistance	R
revolutions per minute	r.p.m.
root mean square	r.m.s.
time	t
torque	T
volt	v.
watt	w.

www.ingramcontent.com/pod-product-compliance
Lightning Source LLC
Chambersburg PA
CBHW082213300426
44117CB00016B/2787